INTRODUCTION TO EDUCATION
Series editor: Jonathan Solity

EMPOWERING PARENTS AND TEACHERS

EMPOWERING PARENTS AND TEACHERS

Working for Children

Sheila Wolfendale

with contributions by Alwyn Morgan, Ray
Phillips, Sue Miller, Jean Robinson, Ann
Evans, Audrey Evans, Hugh Waller, Marsha
Grime, Lynda Pearce

CASSELL

Cassell
Villiers House   387 Park Avenue South
41/47 Strand   New York, NY 10016–8810
London WC2N 5JE, England   USA

First published 1992

British Library Cataloguing-in-Publication Data
A catalogue record for this book is available from the British Library.

ISBN 0–304–32381–0 hardback
     0–304–32380–2 paperback

Typeset by Colset Private Limited, Singapore
Printed and bound in Great Britain by
Biddles Ltd, Guildford and King's Lynn

CONTENTS

v

Contents

EXERCISES

FOREWORD

The 1980s and 1990s have witnessed unprecedented changes to the education system. These have had a dramatic impact, particularly in relation to:

- schools' relationships with parents and the community;
- the funding and management of schools;
- the curriculum;
- the assessment of children's learning.

It can be an extremely daunting task for student teachers to unravel the details and implications of these initiatives. This Introduction to Education series therefore offers a comprehensive analysis and evaluation of educational theory and practice in the light of recent developments.

The series examines topics and issues of concern to those entering the teaching profession. Major themes representing a spectrum of educational opinion are presented in a clear, balanced and analytic manner.

The authors in the series are authorities in their field. They emphasize the need to have a well-informed and critical teaching profession and present a positive and optimistic view of the teacher's role. They endorse the view that teachers have a significant influence over the extent to which any legislation or ideology is translated into effective classroom practice.

Each author addresses similar issues, which can be summarized as:

- presenting and debating theoretical perspectives within appropriate social, political, and educational contexts;
- identifying key arguments;

- identifying individuals who have made significant contributions to the field under review;
- discussing and evaluating key legislation;
- critically evaluating research and highlighting implications for classroom practice;
- providing an overview of the current state of debate within each field;
- describing the features of good practice.

The books are written primarily for student teachers. However, they will be of interest and value to all those involved in education.

Jonathan Solity
Series Editor

Note

In May 1992 the former Department of Education and Science (DES) became the Department for Education (DFE). Most references in this book to that Department are retrospective ones, hence the use of the initials 'DES' in most cases.

CHAPTER 1

Parents as a force in education: describing the purpose and scope of the book

Why write a book about parents in this series? Simply because parents in education are now a force to be reckoned with. In the last twenty or so years, parents have become established on the educational scene, their presence routine in many schools and classrooms, with parental representation on all governing bodies. Research and practice have demonstrated how effective parents are in supporting their children's learning and well-being. The evidence is available from personal testimony from parents, teachers, children, from surveys, questionnaires, case histories, from the results of many projects.

This book has a number of purposes:

- It aims to bring to readers' attention the influence of parents on their children's development and learning.
- It describes some of the initiatives in home–school relations of recent years.
- It considers the factors that encourage an effective working relationship between parents and teachers.
- It examines how that working relationship can be maintained and extended.
- It puts these developments into contemporary contexts and in relation to educational legislation.
- Finally, it attempts to look positively towards the future in terms of home–school links.

SCOPE OF THE BOOK

The plan is to look at the contribution and influence of parents from as many angles as possible, rather as one might look into a prism and see different lights and colours refracted simultaneously. Some of the significant angles the book will examine will be:

- looking into how parents *act* as parents; what they do; what their role is;
- seeing how parents create caring environments at home that provide the contexts to children's development and learning;
- illustrating how parents have become a presence and a force within education and schools;
- looking at the kinds of contact between parents and teachers;
- examining the experience and skills parents bring to joint enterprises with teachers;
- exploring some of the issues to do with sharing responsibility for decisions.

The subject matter of this book encompasses the whole age-range. The major principles apply universally, but examples will be drawn from pre-school to school-leaving age, and will therefore illustrate the unique or distinctive features of collaborative work between parents and teachers at different ages and stages.

A particular feature of this book is the case studies, first-hand descriptions of recent and current work in home–school links and parental involvement. These make up the final two chapters of the book and are written by practitioners who are directly involved in these initiatives. While many examples are peppered throughout the book, the clearest confirmation of the power of these joint ventures comes from this first-hand testimony.

The underpinning philosophy of this book needs to be stated at the outset. As its author I am pleased to reiterate a long-held commitment to the fostering and furtherance of effective, supportive working relationships between home and school, on behalf of and in the interests of children and in pursuit of their fundamental right to quality education by all means and resources available, including the best resource of all, that of the adults in their lives.

Those of us who have been involved over a number of years with a range of parental-involvement projects can attest to the fact that such experiences and insights are hard-won, not easily come by without setbacks, disagreement or fallow periods where little progress and change seems to be being achieved. Yet the successes vindicate the setbacks and so all the efforts are worthwhile in the longer term.

There is now a considerable body of references to the British work on parental involvement which spans the last fifteen or so years. A number of lessons have been learned from this accumulated and still accumulating experience, and what many of the workers in this field have in common is a commitment to a number of key principles:

2

These principles thread their way throughout the book but are briefly defined below to set the scene.

Rights

Parents have fundamental rights to be participant in some (but evidently not all) educational decision-making (for example, in special-needs assessment), via representation on schools' governing bodies, to receive reports from schools about their children's educational progress. The concept of rights can act as a springboard for ensuring not only that parents know their rights but that they can guarantee that these rights will have expression.

Equality

The concept of parents as partners has been addressed by many writers, researchers, practitioners and parents. The issues will be explored in this book. Suffice to say at this stage that the bedrock principle is equal status between parents and professionals, with dialogue between adults who have a common and vested interest in children, given that each brings different but equivalent experience and expertise to that joint enterprise.

Reciprocity

The principle here is that all involved stand to gain from a productive discourse on behalf of children: the children themselves, their parents – whose own rights and interests are represented – and teachers. On the principle of equality identified above, reciprocal involvement rests on the premise that each person involved is contributing and sharing information, expertise and ultimately the responsibility for actions and decisions. Thus accountability belongs to all.

Empowerment

Educational initiatives involving parents must be perceived in their eyes to be benefiting them as described above, but also in terms of the opportunities such involvement provides for parents themselves to learn, to grow, to explore possibilities, to become familiar with organizations such as schools and local education authorities, and to become enabled and confident not only to work within these systems, but, as appropriate and where necessary, to challenge existing structures and traditions. Empowerment usually refers to the means as well as the ends of realizing and expressing wants, needs and rights and of ensuring that the parental voice is heard and has influence.

So the key concepts for this chapter are:

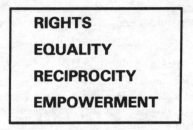

RIGHTS

EQUALITY

RECIPROCITY

EMPOWERMENT

Key concepts will be presented within each chapter and will help to convey the messages inherent in the themes and topics that each chapter aims to present.

Another feature of the book is the exercises in each chapter, which readers can do individually or in a small group. The task will be either a reflective exercise, encouraging thinking about an issue, or a practical exercise, which also involves the reader in thinking and in having ideas and proposing strategies to answer or explore particular issues. The basic purpose of the exercises is to provide stimulus for personal thinking or group discussion on issues that are relevant to most people's experience, such as having parents, going to school, being a parent or a teacher and having responsibility for children's education and welfare. Each exercise follows a format comprising Purpose, What to do, and Comments, and so takes the reader through a process. The reason why the number of exercises varies from chapter to chapter is that some themes and topics lend themselves more readily to practical or reflective tasks. For example, Chapter 6 contains the highest number of exercises, since 'Communication' is fundamental to teacher–parent co-operation. The first such exercise occurs at this point in the chapter, and it is a practical exercise.

EXERCISE: The relevance of the reader's perspective.

Purpose: The idea is to encourage the reader at the outset to reflect on the personal experience that s/he brings to the enterprise of teaching and particularly to gauge the impact and influence that parents and other significant adults have had at key stages of development and events in childhood.

What to do: Have a go at your own 'time line': draw a vertical or horizontal line on a sheet of paper and plot along the line significant events in your own life (choose your own intervals between events); these will include personal, domestic, emotional, educational, academic, professional and career happenings of importance to you. Then, for each of these stages or events, consider the part that those who most cared for you, but especially your parents, have played. This will help to stimulate your thinking as to the impact they had

at different times and the support, understanding or otherwise you
felt they gave.

Comments: Such an appraisal from a personal standpoint will be a
stimulus to considering not only what parents and other significant
adults bring to children's development and education, but also how
the teachers' role complements these aspects.

Each chapter concludes with a Further Reading section, which con-
fines itself to three or so texts which further illuminate or expand the
topic, and/or contain theory and practice ideas on the specific topic. A
brief description accompanies each such reference.

CHAPTER SUMMARY

**This initial chapter has set out the purpose and scope of the book,
presented and defined key concepts that will inform discussion
throughout the book and encouraged readers to identify at first hand
with the subject matter, namely the relationships between parents,
teacher and children.**

FURTHER READING

These three references provide an introduction to the area of home-
school links and parental involvement, as they each describe recent
and current work.

Department of Education and Science (1991) *Parents and Schools:
Aspects of Parental Involvement in Primary and Secondary Schools.*
London: DES. This HMI report describes and comments on the ways
thirty-two primary and thirty-eight secondary schools responded
and involved parents during 1989–90.
Jowett, S., Baginsky, M. and MacNeil, M. M. (1991) *Building Bridges:
Parental Involvement in Schools.* Windsor: NFER-Nelson. Information is obtained via a survey from most LEAs about the forms of
parental involvement practised in schools, and eleven schools or
schemes are chosen for detailed study.
Wolfendale, S. (ed.) (1989) *Parental Involvement: Developing Networks between School, Home and Community.* London: Cassell.
Each chapter describes a different approach to involving parents, in a
number of schools and LEA settings, from pre-school to secondary.

CHAPTER 2

The advent of parents in education: a review of recent developments

CHAPTER OVERVIEW

This chapter aims to chart the arrival and impact of parents in education, and to describe a number of significant recent and current developments which epitomize parental involvement. The contemporary legislative context constitutes a frame for examining the potential for continued parental involvement, and a number of key issues are identified.

AN HISTORICAL PERSPECTIVE

In textbooks on the history of education, parents are conspicuously absent: they appear to exist only in relation to their primary legal duty to send children to school. As state-provided education became more and more widespread throughout this century, parents were never encouraged to linger in schools after depositing their children, usually at the school gates, and the now notorious sign 'NO PARENTS BEYOND THIS POINT' was a commonplace sight.

A number of texts chronicle the arrival of parents on the educational scene (Craft *et al.*, 1980; Wolfendale, 1983) and in particular the advent of parents in school and of increasing links between parents and professionals in a number of spheres. The text by Wolfendale (1983) draws attention to and synthesizes a number of recommendations in several government reports on education and child health which call for closer working links between parents and professionals on the grounds that this is in children's best interests.

The 1970s saw a significant increase in parental involvement activity, which is documented in more detail below, but at this point it is worth asking what was the impetus and spur to this exploration of hitherto uncharted territory. The textbooks cite a number of influences, the most prominent of which was the impact of the American Head Start programme (see Wolfendale, 1983, Chapter 5; Schweinhart and Weikart, 1980/1), a government-sponsored early-intervention programme directed at young socially disadvantaged children and their families. In many of the projects parental involvement in a variety of forms was paramount, and while debate has raged during the last twenty to thirty years over the longer-term effectiveness of Head Start (Woodhead, 1987), nevertheless its methods and practices have been very influential. For example, through the process of becoming and staying part of an early education programme in which their children were participant, many parents became more knowledgeable, more confident, more understanding of the system and better equipped to ask questions and challenge the status quo – in a word, they became empowered (Cochran, 1986). There have been British parallels to this form of community and parent-focused action, which are referred to later.

Through the processes of involvement mentioned above, researchers discovered the effectiveness of parents as educators and trainers across a range of early learning and behaviour change opportunities (Topping, 1986), primarily at home, but at school too. We can see, then, that research and practice in this area have combined to provide not only the 'proof' about the effectiveness of such collaboration, but also its underpinning philosophy and rationale.

THE RATIONALE FOR PARENTAL INVOLVEMENT: A RÉSUMÉ

This list is a combination of initial premises underlying parent-teacher and parent–professional projects and the findings from such work – in other words it is a blend of conviction and practice:

- All parents care about their children's welfare and well-being. There is sufficient evidence that the tiny minority of parents who appear not to care are those who at the time are overwhelmed by stressful life-events and financial pressures, and whose own experience of schooling was not positive enough for them to overcome fears and anxieties about school and teachers. The premise 'all parents care . . .' is the spur to action by teachers and others to find ways for encouraging and welcoming traditionally indifferent parents into a partnership.
- Parents want to do what they believe to be in their child's best interests. Teachers and other professionals have capitalized on this latent good will when inviting parents to be participants in projects.

- Parents want to co-operate. This fundamental premise lies at the heart of many joint endeavours, though the reality is that at any one time parents may be reluctant to make a commitment or find the time, or be too preoccupied with other matters to take a home–school venture on board.
- Parents will respond to invitations to participate in school if they can see the benefit to their child. Similar to the 'good will' premise is the fact that parents' interest in and commitment to their own children overrides an altruistic interest in education and other children's welfare. It is therefore an acceptable springboard to parental involvement.
- Parents are the primary educators of their children and are experts on their children. This is more than axiomatic, the basic premise being that as we know this to be the case (and we can back this up with research evidence as and when we need to) we can make better use of these parental skills and experience than we have done to date.
- Parent and teacher skills complement one another. The evidence is that what parents and teachers bring to joint enterprises is a set of different but complementary skills, perspectives and insights.
- Parents often have vital information and insights concerning their children. This is a truism, admittedly, but the point here is that teachers and other professionals have not made the best use of these. The parents' views have hitherto been confined to annual parents' evenings or the case conference setting, which is limiting and at which parents are often outnumbered by professionals. These are not conducive circumstances for the effective sharing of information and concerns.

  The final two points concern parents' rights to be involved, and these have been fundamental to many of the parent–professional initiatives.
- Involvement of parents should include decision-making, not simply information giving.
- All parents have a right to be involved and to contribute.

A REVIEW OF DEVELOPMENTS IN PARENTAL INVOLVEMENT

A number of writers, some of them involved first hand in projects, have described their and others' work (examples include Wolfendale, 1983; Bastiani, 1988; Stacey, 1991). Yet others have attempted to represent in succinct ways the many activities comprising parental involvement, particularly in schools. For instance, Wolfendale (1992) shows the Wheel of Parental Involvement, which segments the activities into four sections – parents into school; linking with home; written communication; forums for meetings – within which they are represented as the spokes of the wheel. Another way of representing these activities is to list practical suggestions and possibilities, as Long has done (1986).

No published text can do justice to the myriad of local initiatives in the United Kingdom, many of which constitute routine practice and may not even be written up for local consumption, let alone national. One reason for including a number of case studies at the end of this book is to do justice to some of the local work which provides the bed-rock experience in parent–teacher co-operation. However, an attempt is made here to convey to the reader some indication of the most notable developments in recent years. Below is an overview of the major areas, with selected descriptive references. This listing also provides a 'trailer' to the rest of this book, as most of the areas are explored in more detail in subsequent chapters.

Major areas of parental involvement during the 1970s and 1980s: examples and sources

Parents coming into school

Parents assisting with reading and other curriculum areas, and working alongside teachers (Wolfendale, 1989; Stacey, 1991).

Parents as educators at home

Parental involvement in reading (Topping and Wolfendale, 1985); parental involvement in maths (Merttens and Vass, 1990).

Home–school links

Written communication (Atkin and Bastiani, 1988); home–school councils (Templeton, 1989); home visiting (Jowett *et al.*, 1991, Chapter 6).

Community education

School–community links (Grant, 1989); community education (Allen *et al.*, 1987).

Parents as governors and managers

Parent governors (Sallis, 1988).

Parents and special educational needs

Parental involvement in assessment (Wolfendale, 1988); parents, teachers and the 1981 Education Act (Solity and Raybould, 1988).

9

Parental representation: local and national

National groups (ACE, CASE, NCPTA – addresses in end-of-chapter references); special needs parents' groups (Wolfendale, 1989, Chapter 8).

International dimensions to parental involvement

With the single European market fully operational from the beginning of 1993 and with international communications systems making instant contact possible, it is apposite to consider the wider context into which UK work falls. The American experience was briefly chronicled earlier in this chapter. Foundations such as the Bernard Van Leer Foundation have funded many community and home–school initiatives all over the world, notably in developing countries, where schooling may be neither universal nor compulsory, and where consequently there is a high premium on maximizing the parental role. For an earlier account of such initiatives see Wolfendale (1983); for recent international perspectives on home–school and community links see Beattie (1985), Macbeth (1989), Poster and Kruger (1990).

Doubt and dissent

The portrayal of what has undoubtedly become a significant trend in education should not be presented as if there were always consensus or unanimity about the place of parents in schools. Many projects had to fight to become established, many teachers were wary of parents' intrusion into their domain and suspicious of parents' intentions; likewise parents have not always been receptive to invitations to come into school, or participate in school–home learning projects.

All of us involved in various projects over the years can confirm that there is a continuum of teachers' attitudes, epitomized at one end by actual hostility towards parents working in schools and at the other end by a commitment to initiating and sustaining joint work in which parents are perceived as partners. The case studies at the end of this book typify this latter, positive response, but, at the same time, each of the case study authors would attest to the fact that the achievements have not been accomplished without difficulty – and how could it be otherwise when new territory is being explored?

Attitudes and awareness

Some teachers' hostile and negative attitudes are explicable and grounded in a number of legitimate concerns, chief among which are:

- that parents in the classroom will undermine teachers' professionalism;

- that parents' views are not necessarily well informed and there-fore a clash with teachers may be inevitable;
- that the active parents are a vocal, self-selecting group who are not representative of all parents.

In the zeal to involve and empower parents within education, sensi-tivity towards issues of perennial concern to teachers such as status, control and scarcity of resources must be paramount.

Increased awareness and more knowledge are empowering for par-ents and teachers alike. A number of ways of increasing awareness and encouraging the reappraisal of attitudes have been and are being explored. For example, the then Department of Education and Science (DES) commissioned a survey into parental awareness of school educa-tion, carried out during 1989 (DES, 1989), the data from which were to assist the DES to ensure that parents understood, if not actually sup-ported, the many reforms and changes associated with the 1988 Educa-tion Reform Act (ERA). Another project, based at Exeter University (Hughes *et al.*, 1990), aims to explore parents' knowledge about and attitudes to the National Curriculum, assessment, standards and opting out. Initial findings from the first phase of this project reveal that parents are much more positive about their children's schools and teachers than is often realized or acknowledged. Yet another current study based at the Open University, being carried out by Glatter and co-workers, is researching into the reciprocal nature of parental choice; that is, factors governing parents' choice of a school, and responses by schools to such choices.

It is alleged that the most effective point at which to encourage teachers to think about and form constructive attitudes towards work-ing with parents is the initial training stage. Atkin and Bastiani (1988) carried out a survey which explored the extent to which teachers in training were being prepared to work with parents. Their findings con-firmed a diversity of practice, but also a growing awareness and acknowledgement that this phase of preparation for teaching is crucial for the formation not only of attitudes, but of appropriate and effective methodologies for embracing the parental and community dimension in schooling.

Lessons learned from experience

Many of the projects report upon their findings, and readers are urged to follow up these reports at source. What we have learned overall is that there are a number of fundamental requisites that increase the likelihood of a programme's lasting, even if its permanent existence cannot be guaranteed. These include:

- commitment;
- clearly identified aims;

- explicit short-term and longer-term goals;
- mix of 'top-down, bottom-up' decision-making;
- availability of a range of training strategies;
- availability of supporting materials and resources;
- regular review points;
- periodic evaluation by all participants;
- record-keeping that is integral to the programme;
- willingness to be flexible and adapt to changing circumstances.

THE CONTEMPORARY PERSPECTIVE: WHERE ARE WE NOW?

The rationale for parental involvement rests on a number of premises and precursors, as the earlier part of this chapter has attempted to demonstrate. The broader societal backcloth to educational innovation always needs to be taken into account, as the reality is that politics and social forces affect education very directly (Ball, 1990), and during the last decade or so the British political parties have all publicly subscribed to increasing parental rights and representations. Notwithstanding the fact that each party conceives of parental rights and choices from a differing ideological standpoint, it is evident that each woos the electorate with promises of greater involvement and increased status within education.

The Conservative government, in power since 1979, has had the greatest opportunity to translate its promises into reality. Each of the education Acts of Parliament during the last few years has contained key sections outlining rights and choices for parents. Naturally there is considerable ideological debate and disagreement about the nature of choice (open-ended, forced or illusory choice) and the extent of the powers that parents, via a number of mechanisms, can exercise.

Education Acts and parents' rights

There have been five education Acts in a space of twelve years. Let us see what main parental rights have been enshrined in the legislation:

- *1980* Parent representation on governing bodies; choice of school; LEA to provide information about schools.
- *1981* On special educational needs: parents can refer children for assessment; parents' rights to be consulted and kept informed by the school over concerns about their child; parents' right to contribute to assessment; parents' right to appeal against educational placement decision.
- *1986* Right to: receive information from the school; receive an annual report from governors; be invited to an annual meeting called by the governors.
- *1988* Parental choice of school – 'open enrolment'; right to

'opt out' of LEA control, given a sufficient parental voting majority; right to receive annual report on their child's progress in school and with the National Curriculum; right to be informed about the results of assessment.

- *1992* Parents' views to be taken on board as part of the revised inspection of schools procedures; publication of schools' assessment results and attendance rates.

A dual philosophy appears to run through these five pieces of legislation. On the one hand the educational process is opened up for parents; they gain access to hitherto arcane and at worst secretive decision-making; they appear to have genuine choice in respect of educational spending (remember, parents are represented on governing bodies, which in turn are responsible for the delivery of the National Curriculum). These rights increase the accountability to parents of teachers and educational administrators. On the other hand, schooling is now so regulated at each phase that individual parents might find it difficult to penetrate the thicket of National Curriculum and assessment arrangements to seek redress for any grievance they might have. Furthermore, with the advent of Local Management of Schools (LMS), and the consequent fragmentation of local education authorities as their financial authority is eroded and then probably removed, what champions fighting their cause could parents have?

The question posed at the start of this section was, 'Where are we now?', and it was intended that this part would be a stock-taking of parental involvement to date. The legislation is more positive than negative, and on the whole is conducive to the continuation of many initiatives that have been started and maintained over the last few years. Indeed, there is evidence that we are moving into new phases of parental involvement, very much consolidating the work that has gone before and responding to opportunities conferred by the legislation. These new opportunities will be explored in later chapters. Suffice it to announce at this point, by way of a trailer, that we shall be considering the potential in:

- consulting parents as part of school development and review processes;
- all schools having written and active policies on parental involvement;
- parents and teachers writing and abiding by a home–school agreement;
- parents being routinely involved in assessment.

FUNDAMENTAL ISSUES: IS THERE A BLUEPRINT?

It might occur to those teachers or teachers in training who have not yet had much chance to initiate or participate in home–school initiatives to ask whether there is a formula for successful operation of such ventures. There cannot be; research and practice to date can only provide us with exemplars and inspiration and, on the basis of hard-won insights and experiences, identify the prerequisites for success without being able to guarantee it (see the list earlier in this chapter).

The teachers and parents in each school, even each class, evolve their own blueprint and find a niche in which they feel comfortable working together. However, the least ambitious and the most ambitious schemes have in common the fact that all parental involvement work has at some point to address some fundamental issues to do with creating opportunities for all parents to participate, with what the boundaries of such involvement are to be, and with how the participants share what powers are available. A number of key concepts relating to some of these fundamental issues are identified below, with key sources, and then elaborated and discussed:

> **INVOLVEMENT versus PARTNERSHIP (Pugh, 1989)**
>
> **PARENT POWER (Wragg, 1989)**
>
> **EQUAL OPPORTUNITIES (Tomlinson, 1987)**

Involvement versus partnership

Reams have been written about the distinction between these two concepts, and a number of writers have attempted definitions based on first-hand participation in various projects (Wolfendale, 1983; Mittler and McConachie, 1983). Wolfendale (1983) identified partnership as characterized by parents being:

- active and central in decision-making and its implementation;
- perceived as having equal strengths and equivalent expertise;
- able to contribute to as well as receive services (reciprocity);
- able to share responsibility so that they and professionals are mutually accountable (p. 15).

Pugh (1989) defines partnership as 'a working relationship that is characterized by a shared sense of purpose, mutual respect and the willingness to negotiate. This implies a sharing of information, responsibility, skills, decision-making and accountability' (p. 5).

It is evident that there are few home–school projects that fulfil these criteria of partnership, and indeed, with no history of community and 'consumer' participation in the erstwhile closed world of schools, we have little tradition to draw upon to bring about partnership. The very concept challenges the long-standing supremacy and autonomy of headteachers. However, it may be a propitious time to suggest that partnership *is* possible, since some of the recent educational legislation referred to above is conducive to the maximum participation in educational decision-making by parents, and creates opportunities for teachers and parents to share on an equal basis. And since powers have devolved to the governing bodies, the parental representation there becomes significant. But the fullest extent of partnership is uncharted territory, and some practitioners prefer the more modest aims of encouraging as much involvement by parents in school life as possible, regarding partnership as an ideal and therefore unattainable.

Parent power

The shifting sands of power-plays and power-sharing maintain partnership with parents as an ideal. The reality is that despite extension of parental rights via legislation, the major powers remain vested in the large institutions of state and local government. The government in the 1988 Education Reform Act emphasizes the consumer approach to education, whereby parents can 'shop around' for 'best buy' schools and can, by applying criteria or performance indicators, judge whether or not the goods (the school) are up to scratch (obtaining enough examination passes, for example). These elements of choice seem like having power, but, as all of us as consumers find, getting redress for bad service or shoddy goods is rarely easy. The Citizen's Charter is undoubtedly an attempt to give consumers a better deal and there are educational corollaries in the Charter, which covers public services.

Wragg (1989) distinguishes between 'rights', which 'represent nothing more than an entitlement', and 'power', which 'is the ability to influence action' (p. 125), and goes on to discuss the ramifications of the distinction. He points out that as by no means all parents possess the requisite knowledge and understanding of the system or the confidence to manipulate it, exercise of what powers parents have remains necessarily limited. Thus, to return to a key concept identified at the outset of this chapter, empowerment by parents on a wide scale is still far from the reality.

As Wragg is one of the first to acknowledge, professionals have rights too, and parents as uninformed laypersons cannot, he feels, play a part in such professional matters as teacher appraisal. This view is clearly at odds with a conservative political view that processes like teacher appraisal ought to be open to scrutiny by local people such as business persons, be they parents or not.

Equal opportunities

Tomlinson has pointed out (1987) that many parents and children from ethnic minority backgrounds continue to be disadvantaged

15

within the educational system for a host of reasons. Accessing ethnic minority parents has been a priority in a number of projects; for example, in the community education work by Coventry LEA (Watts, 1990). This area forms half of Chapter 7 of this book, where the issues will be explored in more depth. But the philosophy and the commitment need to be reiterated at this point; namely, that just as equal opportunities and entitlement to all curriculum and educational opportunities must be extended as of right to all children (and educationalists have to make every effort to ensure that this is so), so must these fundamental rights be extended to all parents too. This means the creation of explicit means to guarantee that information reaches parents (using translators and interpreters if needed), that parents' linguistic competence does not bar them from access to teachers, and that parents are not adversely judged on the basis of differing child-rearing methods and attitudes.

THE FUTURE AGENDA OF PARENTAL INVOLVEMENT

There remains plenty to do! Here are some suggestions:

- consolidate and maintain existing good practice;
- replicate successful projects elsewhere;
- pursue emerging ideas, such as home–school agreement, policy on parental involvement;
- ensure that involving parents is a high priority for schools, at a time when they need allies in the shape of informed, supportive parents;
- explore the boundaries of involvement versus partnership;
- encourage continued research into parental participation.

One seminar on parental involvement held during 1990 identified initial and continuing teacher education as arenas to foster the skills needed for teachers to work effectively and comfortably with parents.

EXERCISE: Appraising parental involvement from your own experience

Purpose: Each of us has memories of our schooldays, including the times when our parents visited school and their reasons for going. The idea is to compare and contrast experiences then with parental involvement nowadays.

What to do:

* Think back to your own schooldays.
* Then consider the extent to which your parents were involved

with schools (visits, contacts, letters, reports, going to concerts, plays, school trips, etc.). List these activities.
* Finally, on your own or in discussion with others, compare home–school links in your own experience with present-day practice. What conclusions do you come to?

Comments: This exercise juxtaposes past personal experience with present personal and professional perspectives, so that progress in this area can be assessed.

CHAPTER SUMMARY

This chapter has sought to present the scope and extent of the many original and imaginative projects of the last few years that come under the banner of parental involvement. In so doing it has provided a trailer for the rest of the book and at the same time raised a number of ideological and educational issues. The legislative context is a relevant backcloth to many of the initiatives and a modest attempt has been made to project a future agenda for the area of parental involvement.

FURTHER READING

Macleod, F. (ed.) (1989) *Parents and Schools: The Contemporary Challenge*. Lewes: Falmer. Each of the twelve contributors examines a different facet of parental involvement, based on first-hand experience. There are chapters on governors, gender and race dimensions, and political aspects to home–school links. This is a discursive, reflective book designed to stimulate debate and discussion.

Stacey, M. (1991) *Parents and Teachers Together*. Milton Keynes: Open University Press. This is a practical handbook about how to involve parents in schools, which examines the problems as well as the opportunities. The key to success is seen to be the interaction between teachers and parents.

Wolfendale, S. (1983) *Parental Participation in Children's Development and Education*. London: Gordon & Breach. This provides a comprehensive account of the origins and scope of many parental involvement projects from pre-school to secondary, within multidisciplinary and international perspectives. A theoretical framework for partnership is proposed.

REFERENCES

Allen, G., Bastiani, J., Martin, I. and Richards, K. (eds) (1987) *Community Education: An Agenda for Educational Reform*. Milton Keynes: Open University Press.

Atkin, J. and Bastiani, J. (1988) Training teachers to work with parents. In J. Bastiani (ed.), *Parents and Teachers*. Vol. 2. *From Policy to Practice*. Windsor: NFER-Nelson.

Ball, S. (1990) *Politics and Policy Making in Education*. London: Routledge.

Bastiani, J. (ed.) (1988) *Parents and Teachers*. Vol. 2. *From Policy to Practice*. Windsor: NFER-Nelson.

Beattie, N. (1985) *Professional Parents. Parent Participation in Four Western European Countries*. Lewes: Falmer.

Cochran, M. (1986) The parental empowerment process: building on family strengths. Chapter 1 in J. Harris (ed.), *Child Psychology in Action*. London: Croom Helm.

Craft, M., Raynor, J. and Cohen, L. (eds) (1980) *Linking Home and School: A New Review*. 3rd edition. London: Harper & Row.

Department of Education and Science. Parental Awareness of School Education. London: DES.

Glatter, R. Parental and School Choice Interaction Study (PASCI). Milton Keynes: Open University, School of Education.

Grant, D. (1989) *Learning Relations*. London: Routledge.

Hughes, M., Wikeley, F. and Nash, T. (1990) *Parents and the National Curriculum. An Interim Report*. Exeter: School of Education, Exeter University.

Jowett, S., Baginsky, M. and MacNeil, M. M. (1991) *Building Bridges. Parental Involvement in Schools*. Windsor: NFER-Nelson.

Long, R. (1986) *Developing Parental Involvement in Primary Schools*. Basingstoke: Macmillan Education.

Macbeth, A. (1989) *Involving Parents. Effective Parent–Teacher Relations*. Oxford: Heinemann Educational.

Merttens, R. and Vass, J. (1990) *Bringing School Home*. London: Hodder & Stoughton.

Mittler, P. and McConachie, H. (eds) (1983) *Parents, Professionals and Mentally Handicapped People*. London: Croom Helm.

Poster, C. and Kruger, A. (eds) (1990) *Community Education in the Western World*. London: Routledge.

Pugh, G. (1989) Parents and professionals in pre-school services: is partnership possible? Chapter 1 in S. Wolfendale (ed.), *Parental Involvement: Developing Networks between School, Home and Community*. London: Cassell.

Sallis, J. (1988) *Schools, Parents and Governors: A New Approach to Accountability*. London: Routledge.

Schweinhart, L. and Weikart, D.P. (1980/1) *Young Children Grow Up: The Effects of the Perry Preschool Program on Youths through Age 15*. High/Scope Monograph. London: Grant McIntyre.

Solity, J. and Raybould, E. (1988) *A Teacher's Guide to Special Needs: A Positive Response to the 1981 Education Act*. Milton Keynes: Open University Press.

Stacey, M. (1991) *Parents and Teachers Together*. Milton Keynes: Open University Press.

Templeton, J. (1989) Creation of a home school council in a secondary school. Chapter 5 in S. Wolfendale (ed.), *Parental Involvement: Developing Networks between School, Home and Community.* London: Cassell.

Tomlinson, S. (1987) Home, school and community. In J. Bastiani (ed.), *Parents and Teachers.* Vol. 1. *Perspectives on Home–School Relations.* Windsor: NFER-Nelson.

Topping, K. (1986) *Parents as Educators.* London: Croom Helm.

Topping, K. and Wolfendale, S. (eds) (1985) *Parental Involvement in Children's Reading.* London: Croom Helm.

Watts, J. (1990) UK: The Community Education Development Centre. Chapter 17 in C. Poster and A. Kruger (eds), *Community Education in the Western World.* London: Routledge.

Wolfendale, S. (1983) *Parental Participation in Children's Development and Education.* London: Gordon & Breach.

Wolfendale, S. (1988) *The Parental Contribution to Assessment.* Developing Horizons No. 10. Coventry: National Council for Special Education (now known as NASEN; National Association for Special Educational Needs).

Wolfendale, S. (ed.) (1989) *Parental Involvement: Developing Networks between School, Home and Community.* London: Cassell.

Wolfendale, S. (1992) *Primary Schools and Special Needs: Policy, Planning and Provision.* 2nd edition. London: Cassell.

Woodhead, M. (1987) Some lessons from research into pre-school effectiveness. *Concern*, Summer.

Wragg, T. (1989) Parent power. Chapter 6 in F. Macleod (ed.), *Parents and Schools: The Contemporary Challenge.* Lewes: Falmer.

ADDRESSES

ACE (The Advisory Centre for Education), 18 Victoria Park Square, London E2 9PB. It runs a telephone help line for parents, publishes many guides to education and speaks on behalf of parents.

CASE (Campaign for the Advancement of State Education). 158 Durham Road. London SW20 0DG. It is committed to free, universal, state-provided education and full parental participation in educational decision-making, and publishes a newsletter and pamphlets.

NCPTA (National Confederation of Parent Teacher Associations), 2 Ebbsfleet Industrial Estate, Stonebridge Road, Gravesend, Kent DA11 9D2. It represents PTAs, has over 9,000 schools in membership, runs a telephone help line, publishes newsletters and pamphlets, and aims to represent teachers' as well as parents' interests.

CHAPTER 3

The parenting role and its relevance to education

CHAPTER OVERVIEW

The spotlight is put on the role and function of parents in children's lives, and on the effects of families on children's development and education. The premise is advanced that teachers and others who work with children, whether or not they also work directly with their parents, need to have an understanding of the place of parents in order to meet children's learning and other needs effectively.

DEFINING PARENTS AND FAMILIES

Thus far in the book, the term 'parents' has been used without definition or qualification. It is appropriate now to spell out the use and conception of parents as a term.

In previous writings (Wolfendale, 1983) it was made explicit that the term is used generically to embrace not only the dictionary definition of a parent as 'one who brings forth or produces' (*Collins, Concise Oxford*) but also the broader sense of a parent figure being the person or persons who has or have care, custody and control over, and concern for, a child. This conception then includes any combination of adult caretakers, and so the use of 'parents' in this book certainly does not imply adherence to a stereotypic conventional nuclear family – for as we know, present-day realities are very different from this outmoded notion of what constitutes a family.

Family contexts

In fact, as Vetere and Gale point out (1987), there has been little research into the family first hand, probably for quite obvious reasons. Family life for all of us is a sacred domain, with relatives and friends entering into the nucleus by invitation, and with professionals such as teachers likewise stepping into a family on that family's terms. So it is not easy to scrutinize the intimate, intricate myriad of interactions and emotions that make up the composition of any family. Traditionally this has mattered only when a child's behaviour or learning is a cause for concern; that is to say, teachers and others involved may hypothesize causes or influences from within the family to explain alleged problems. But the evidence on which these assertions are based is often flimsy, the 'truth' inaccessible, the facts available partial, selective, incomplete. Professionals may be ambivalent, on the one hand not wanting to invade family privacy, yet on the other feeling they need to probe and explore so as to explain, if not justify, the problem in family terms. These comments are a preface to looking more closely at what parents do, on the grounds that home–school links can succeed only if a number of assumptions are dispelled by practitioners from the outset and replaced by better general understanding of family functioning.

As the researchers in a participant observation study of family life, Vetere and Gale (1987), point out, no one theory is able to account for all family facts, nor can professionals such as educational psychologists, educational welfare officers or therapists have the luxury of time to be participant observers 'in these days of public accountability and the search for the holy grail of effective service delivery' (p. 198). At least, however, we need to synthesize the considerable experience and insights of practitioners working with children and sometimes with their families with the findings of researchers who delve into family processes with an objective and analytical eye.

Ecological perspectives on the family

Families have been defined in various ways. One way of perceiving the family is to see it as a social arrangement for the protection and rearing of children. Another is to take on board the three perspectives offered by Kagan (1979); that is, the state's, the parents' and the child's. From the parents' perspective the family can be a 'locus of solace and psychic relief . . . it provides each adult with an opportunity to feel needed and useful . . . it offers parents an opportunity to validate the value system they brought to adulthood' (p. 211). For the child, the family offers a model for identification, a source of protection and target of attachment, a setting wherein he or she will receive information and guidance, a place in which skills can be gradually acquired and competence achieved. This summarizes the 'tasks' that parents undertake when parenting their children, and will be elaborated later in the chapter.

Many dramatic changes in family composition are taking place in contemporary society, forcing a redefinition of the term 'family' to encompass different types of parent ('natural', step, foster, adoptive, single) as well as the notion of a 'reconstituted' family, a coming together of family members via divorce, remarriage or cohabitation. Contemporary understanding of the place of the family within society, based on much research, is that, as a system, it is 'nested' within other systems and organizations within society. This is the *ecological* perspective, which has been defined thus by Bronfenbrenner (1979), who is acknowledged to be influential in this area:

> the ecology of human development involves the scientific study of the progressive, mutual accommodation between an active, growing human being and the changing properties of the immediate setting in which the developing person lives, as this process is affected by relations between these settings and by the larger contexts in which the settings are embedded. (p. 21)

To explain this further: a child's home and family is his/her microsystem, embedded within larger systems (macrosystems) comprising school, clubs, the wider family, network of friends and so on. The practical implication of this way of conceiving the place of children in their various spheres of activity is that the differing and relative influences on children as they grow can be assessed.

For more information on ecological perspectives, see work by Wolfendale (1992, Appendix 5) and Thomas (1992).

The family as an educational environment and a place of learning

Considerable research has taken place on how children learn at home, how they communicate with family members and how relationships are formed. Some of the work parallels research into how children learn and communicate in school, and we can see the relative influences, therefore, on children's development. The information can be subjected to several levels of interpretation:

- It can confirm knowledge based on our own experience and observation, and therefore our deductive 'common sense'; that is, it provides further evidence to us that parents and families are indeed influential on children's language, social, emotional and intellectual development.
- It provides scientific verification of what we experience and observe incidentally by using systematic hypothesis-testing methods and fine-grained techniques of analysis.
- It sheds light on the minutiae of the complex processes of

acquiring language, becoming a communicator, developing socialization skills and learning to solve problems.

Child development textbooks usually include sections on the influence of the family and the writers attempt to conceptualize this massive area. For example, Grotevant (1989) postulates four levels of analysis of the influences and effects of the family upon child development: the individual; dyadic relationships within the family; the whole-family system; and the interface of the family and its contexts. This approach is compatible with the ecological framework outlined above. In another text, Berk (1989) lists five functions of the family which we need to understand in order to appraise their influences upon children's development: reproduction; economic services; societal order; socialization; and emotional support. Berk briefly traces the evolution of the family over time, pointing to the lesson from history that the concept and purpose of the family do not stay static; the family unit is responsive to external pressures, changes within society, and political ideology concerning the family, maternal role, etc. It is true that teachers and other educationalists can do little to effect change on a grand scale to benefit children, but it is suggested that it is at least helpful for teachers to conceptualize and acknowledge the relative influences upon children, to take on board the findings from research and absorb these into their pedagogical strategies.

For example, Dunn (1989) asserts that 'research indicates that the familiar world of the family, and especially conversation with an affectionate parent, provide contexts of especial value for very young children's intellectual development' (p. 78). The research evidence she cites is that of Tizard and Hughes (1984), which revealed much about the discourse between parent and young child, as well as her own and colleagues' research into the development of children's understanding of feelings, motives and social rules. Dunn concludes that there are four major features of family interactions that may contribute to the learning that takes place:

- the emotional significance of family interactions;
- discourse about cause and consequence;
- children's pleasure in mastery over the social world;
- the focused, individual nature of interactions at home.

We can see a number of parallels here with school-based learning: some aspects of home-based learning are clearly integral to interactions and opportunities that school provides. The point here is that we must not lose sight of the unique characteristics of the different, though complementary, settings in which children learn. The following chapter picks up on a number of these key themes.

We turn now to look more specifically at what parents do, to examine their role and function, and to see what child-rearing styles there are.

The premise is that increased understanding about these processes will enable teachers not only to appraise the influences upon children but also to communicate effectively with parents from a baseline of knowledge.

PARENTS: THEIR ROLE, FUNCTION AND ACTIVITIES

First of all, let us acknowledge the universality of the experience of being parented (remember, the definition of 'parents' at the outset of this chapter was broad). Later in this chapter there is an exercise which encourages readers to reflect upon their experience of being parented. The notion of 'parents' impinges upon all our lives and we each hold not only our own notion and understanding of what parents do, based primarily on our own experience, but a corresponding model of what a good parent is.

This examination of parenting will be presented in four different ways or, better still, *levels*:

- practical;
- moral/abstract;
- conceptual;
- empirical

Practical

The practical level is defined in terms of our own practical experience of having been parented and reared. This is the strongest influence on our own thinking and attitudes about parenting; on the basis of this experience, we tend to internalize models and styles of parenting, develop our own ideas as to what constitutes a good parent, and appraise the extent to which we consider our parents did 'a good job'. Thus the criteria we employ to judge parental effectiveness are based first and foremost on egocentric perspectives, and we can all be subject, from time to time, to strong reactions when evoking our past and the influence of our parents. We carry this inheritance forward to our child-rearing practices, if and when we become parents. Some people model their attitudes and practices on their parents', whether or not this approach is consciously articulated; others consciously or unwittingly reject their parents' approach in favour of an alternative style of child-rearing, based on hypotheses that their preferred practice will be more effective in the long run than the ones they were subjected to. Despite such variations in practice, however, what we all have in common is the parental legacy.

One of the effects of this universal experience is an acceptance that parenthood is a natural state, that being a parent comes naturally, that the skills do not necessarily need to be taught or practised. We shall see later in the chapter that this assumption has been challenged in recent years, and that the idea that one's first-hand, *practical* experience of being parented is necessarily an adequate or sufficient basis on which to be a parent has been questioned.

Moral/abstract

The moral or abstract level of interpreting parenting relates directly to one's own experience, but refers explicitly to the idealized picture we have of the 'good parent'. Irrespective of the quality of parenting we think we experienced, each of us can identify qualities or attributes that comprise good parenting behaviour. Society is imbued with such concepts, which become value judgements with which either to condemn or to praise behaviour by parents. Over time, we internalize models of good parenting and can identify those attributes we think define a good parent. Because these are implicit, then, parents themselves can and do easily feel anxious and guilty that their own parenting behaviour falls short of this ideal blueprint.

The *moral/abstract* label refers to the fact that these matters are internalized more than they are aired and shared, and also that there does exist in people's perceptions a kind of best practice, a moral imperative.

Conceptual

The previous two levels dealt with the received wisdom, society's folklore and assumptions based on the universality of our experience as to what parenting is, as distinct from attempts that have been made by psychologists, child development experts and researchers to formulate ideas as to what parents do. The main characteristic that distinguishes the third, conceptual, level of considering parenting from the previous two is that it is a *descriptive* approach, not an exhortatory one. That is, it describes what parents actually do without positing what they *should* do in order to be 'good' parents. Thus the emphasis is on the goals, functions and styles of parenting. These processes are explored below.

Empirical

The empirical level is in the domains of scientific endeavour and research enquiry. Painstaking observation (using camera and video aids as appropriate), meticulous recording and various types of analysis characterize the empirical approach to finding out what parents do. This approach relies on sufficient data from large enough representative samples over periods of time long enough to accumulate the wealth of data needed. One of the earlier pioneers of this way of working was Gesell, who, with colleagues, established a tradition of closely focused, systematic observation of children from birth upwards

(Gesell and Ilg, 1965). This method has been an integral feature of American research into child behaviour, child–child and parent–child interaction ever since, and has formed a key part of the longitudinal studies in parent behaviour of Kagan (1984) and Burton White (1978).

BECOMING A PARENT

Irrespective of the age when someone becomes a parent, this event is acknowledged to be a highly significant part of the lifespan (Lefrancois, 1990), not the least reason being that many important decisions and changes in lifestyle are made as a consequence. Shaffer (1989) describes the transition to parenthood, identifying changes in role, habits, perceptions and expectations. There are of course huge individual differences in the extent to which parents-to-be and parents conceive of and articulate their parenting goals, and likewise differences in their expressed intentions as to how they plan to rear their child(ren). Shaffer (1989) describes the phasing of parental priorities:

> Parents and other caregivers are initially concerned about maximising the child's chances of survival, and higher-order goals such as teaching the child to talk, count or abide by moral rules are placed on the back burner until it is clear that the youngster is healthy and likely to survive. (p. 562)

The 'transition to parenthood' phase is becoming an object of study, with researchers focusing on key past and current influences, continuing transition as parents go on to have more than one child, and the effects of family support programmes on new parents (Michaels and Goldberg, 1988, where the table on pp. 352–3, 'Phases of the transition period', which outlines competency and risk profiles of parenthood, is useful).

WHAT PARENTS DO: LISTING PARENTING FUNCTIONS

In an earlier book (Wolfendale, 1983) an attempt was made to describe a whole range of parenting functions. The purpose then was to provide a conceptual framework for considering what parents do and a stimulus for discussion. This list is reproduced below and is followed by an exercise:

1   provide means of survival (meet 'primary' needs)
2   provide emotional support and endorsement (meet 'secondary' needs)
3   provide the setting in which personal development takes place
4   provide an environment in which exploration and hypothesis-testing take place

5   provide a frame of reference against and in which exploration outside the home can take place
6   provide a protective environment for their young
7   provide opportunities and direction for the growth of independent functioning and self-organization
8   act as models (of language, social/emotional behaviour)
9   train and guide their young towards understanding of and adherence to social norms (controls and restraints)
10   act as possessors and transmitters of knowledge and information about the world
11   act as decision-makers and arbiters of decisions, minute by minute and in the longer term. (p. 155)

EXERCISE: Giving examples of what parents do

Purpose: To match each of the eleven parenting functions above with actual examples of what parents do.

What to do: On your own, or with someone else, or in a small group, go through each of the eleven functions and provide at least one example for each. To help you start this exercise, two examples are given below:

1   provide means of survival
   Example: Ensure children are regularly fed.
6   provide a protective environment for their young
   Example: Minimize the presence of dangerous objects in the home; be vigilant at all times.

Comments: These are examples only – they are not correct answers, as there are none. So do exercise your imagination for this task.

PARENTING STYLES

We turn now to a consideration of differences between parents in attitudes to bringing up children, handling them, responding to their behaviour, training them. Most parents have a recognizable style of interacting with their children which is fairly constant over time, though of course there can be differences between two parents in one family. Identifying and describing such styles is one thing, however; it is another matter to attempt to make connections between particular styles and their apparent short-term or longer-term effects. This is an area potentially fraught with value judgements, as professionals such as teachers can fall into the trap of equating a parenting style with the behaviour a child is manifesting. Outsiders to the intricacies of an individual family unit can make simplistic connections between apparent parental style and apparent child behaviour.

Nor is the research much more helpful in identifying or 'proving' longer-term connections between a particular style and children's behaviour, learning success or adjustment to society, though many attempts have been made; for example, to connect socio-economic status, attitudes to parenting and effects on children (Rutter and Madge, 1976) or to link deviant adolescent behaviour with antecedent parental behaviour. This is not to deny cause and effect where there is, seemingly, more proof – for example, in clinical settings where case studies abound demonstrating connections between parental competence and effects upon children (Polansky *et al.*, 1981).

Both Gross (1989) and Berk (1989) describe in some detail four styles of parenting: overprotective, permissive, authoritarian and authoritative. These authors go on to suggest some connections between the style and the longer-term effects on children's behaviour, but are careful to emphasize that these connections are possible, not definitive.

This exercise is suggested as a means of exploring parenting style:

EXERCISE: Remembering your parents' style of parenting

Purpose: To attempt to recollect and describe your parents' style and to consider its possible effects upon you.

What to do: On your own, initially, remember and describe the parenting style of your parents, or, if this is more applicable, of your mother/father separately. Use the list above as a prompt, but try to think of your own categories in describing your parents' style. Then consider what effects their style of and attitude to parenting might have had upon you.

Comments: This is a reflective and very personal exercise which you may or may not want to share with anyone else. This voyage of discovery or rediscovery is intended to complement your professional perspectives on parenting.

GENDER DIFFERENCES IN PARENTING AND CHILD-REARING

The second half of the twentieth century is proving to be quite momentous in terms of social change and mobility, and of patterns of and opportunities for employment. Increased job opportunities for women have had a significant effect on the traditional conception and role of mothers in particular, though the fathers' role has come under scrutiny too as a corollary of these changes.

Mothers and mothering

The overwhelming majority of studies for many years have focused on mother–child interaction (mothers and children interacted more because they were together more often; mothers were more accessible anyway since fewer worked than fathers: Ainsworth *et al.*, 1991), and on the possible effects on young children of being away from their mothers in some form of day care (Tizard, 1986). The topic of mothers *vis-à-vis* their sons and daughters is bound to be endlessly fascinating, since it touches all our lives and impinges upon so many of our decisions and choices. The significant adjustment required by 'new' mothers to their status and role is explored in Ball (1987), and the construct of 'motherhood' and the acts of mothering are explored in depth in Phoenix *et al.* (1991), which aims to demolish myths about there being an ideal style of mothering and about the alleged effects on children of having a working mother, whether or not she is a single mother.

Fathers and fathering

Although the mother's role and function initially received much more attention in social and developmental research, the balance is being redressed by a number of studies and publications that have explored: effects on fathers of having working partners; the extent to which fathers participate in child care, child-rearing, household chores and routines; and the effects on men of becoming fathers (Beail and McGuire, 1982; McKee and O'Brien, 1982; Lewis, 1986; Lamb, 1987). The assumption that fathers' acceptance of and participation in these new responsibilities has significantly increased is challenged by Lewis and O'Brien (1987).

Nevertheless, professionals who interact with parents – teachers are an example – need to bear in mind not only the effects on children of domestic arrangements where they impinge upon children's behaviour, learning and well-being, but also parents' own perceptions of their role and responsibilities. As traditional role boundaries become eroded, so the stereotypes we have of maternal and paternal behaviour need to be challenged and laid to rest.

CULTURAL DIFFERENCES IN PARENTING AND CHILD-REARING

Comparative views of parenthood confirm a number of cross-cultural universals, as well as features that are highly specific to a culture or race/religion mix. The anthropologist Margaret Mead (Mead and Wolfenstein, 1970) perceived all children in all cultures as *learners* who acquire universal skills such as walking, eating, talking and who learn particular and unique skills provided they have the opportunity to do so. As she says, 'humanity . . . is a matter . . . of our capacity to accumulate and build upon the inventions and experience of previous generations (quoted in Wolfendale, 1983, p. 153). Thus, parents' or indeed adults' responsibility is to provide the circumstances in which the learning can take place, as well as to equip children to be adaptable to societal changes so that, as Tucker (1977) put it, 'the universals of childhood become transformed by social conditions' (p. 14).

In a multicultural, pluralistic society the challenge becomes one of juxtaposing the developmental 'universals' which most children acquire against the unique and highly particular circumstances in which all child-rearing takes place. Family practices in preparing and eating food, disciplining children and training them socially are undertaken within and are part of the family frame of reference, based on parents' own upbringing (see earlier in the chapter), their societal/cultural inheritance and possibly their religious routines and customs. Sensitivity to individual family differences is paramount if we are all to avoid charges of, at worst, *racist* responses, simply because teachers and other professionals find it very difficult to be adequately informed about and understand a range of child-rearing practices and attitudes. The Commission for Racial Equality (1989) offers a practical guide to race equality and child care, and has this to say about child-rearing practices:

> Norms about childrearing practices have often been formulated without much consideration for ethnic differences. Where there is an emphasis on developmental 'stages' the use of ethnocentric judgements may lead to some children being labelled as 'culturally deprived' . . . it is possible that parents with different childrearing traditions may be judged to be inadequate parents . . . Perceived lack of concern for strict bedtimes, for example, may be a failure to acknowledge the importance placed by a family on being together in the evenings rather than being separated by defined bedtimes. Or when children are collected by different family members at the end of the day, such arrangements may be condemned as failing to give the child a proper sense of consistency or security. What may not be recognised here is that these children come from families where several members, all of whom they trust, care for them and share the responsibility for meeting them. There is no single 'best' way to bring up a child, and there are as many differences in childrearing practices among white and among black families as there are between them. (pp. 22, 23)

The implication of the CRE's strictures is that professionals need to reappraise assessment and communication techniques in order to elicit information free from their own bias, values and constructions.

PREPARING FOR AND RESPONDING TO PARENTHOOD

The idea that the skills involved in being an effective parent are 'natural', instinctive and universal has been challenged in recent years by some writers and researchers, who have suggested that preparation for parenthood be an integral part of the school curriculum at secondary level (Whitfield, 1980; Pugh and De'Ath, 1984). In fact this is the case in many schools, but its provision varies from school to school and LEA to LEA. In some schools, parenthood classes form part of a life skills approach; in others the topic is seen to be intrinsic to personal and social education (PSE). What is lacking is a national consensus about the importance of this topic, which is necessary for awareness and training to form part of an agreed syllabus undertaken by all children.

The premises underlying such an approach would be:

- Most people do become parents; thus the subject's relevance is readily apparent.
- No skill is instinctive: all have to be learnt, practised and used.
- Preparation, in the form of awareness and knowledge, would increase the chances that children would come to the state of parenthood better informed and therefore more competent.

The last point is really a hypothesis waiting to be tested. Since we have never had a national campaign nor an agreed syllabus, we cannot yet know whether such a preparation would in fact make any difference to readiness or improved skills in being a parent; nor can we know what the effects would be upon parent–child relationships and child behaviour.

In part because this area is not a mandatory school curriculum area and because teachers do not receive an adequate training or preparation themselves to teach something that is still optional, there have been programmes developed that come under the description of parent education. These programmes, targeted at existing parents, aim to support their parental endeavours and improve certain parenting skills and parental confidence, and in so doing to benefit children directly too (Pugh and Poulton, 1987). The practice and the methodology are particularly advanced in the United States of America (Powell, 1988; Fine, 1989). Since many of these programmes come under the broad umbrella of intervention approaches with children and parents, this topic is explored further in the following chapter.

SUPPORTING PARENTS

In the UK there are a number of examples of ways in which guidance and support for parents are offered, both targeted and untargeted. The latter include the many 'baby books' that can be found in bookshops and even chemists', which offer advice to parents from conception onwards, through pregnancy and birth and on to rearing babies and toddlers (Kohner, 1986). The premise underlying such support is

31

summed up in the words of one of the books (Health Education Council, 1989): 'No one needs a book to tell them what's good about being a parent. Parents turn to books when they need information, when they're worried, when they've got questions or worries, small or large. This is a book you can turn to' (from the front page).

Another source of untargeted support, aimed at any parents who come across the books and feel that they could benefit from general advice, is the manuals which deal with behaviour and a whole range of the minor as well as major child-rearing problems that can crop up in any home (Gross, 1989; Woolfson, 1989; Yapp, 1991). For a critique of 'baby books' and the mixed blessings they offer, see Wolfendale (1983, Chapter 9).

Targeted support includes courses on child development for parents where real-life issues can be explored directly (Harris, 1986), as well as specific programmes available for any parents who wish to enrol on them, such as those run by the Parent Network (Sokolov and Hutton, 1988), which describes itself as 'a support organisation for parents offering new ways to meet the challenges of family life'. Parents link with each other through Parent-Link and, via a mix of practical approaches based on sound theoretical principles, are empowered to reappraise their attitudes to becoming and being parents, to develop their skills and to offer support to other parents.

What untargeted and targeted approaches have in common is the acknowledgement that parenthood is a mix of joys and stresses, and is even subject to what Procaccini and Kiefaber (1983) refer to as 'parent burnout'.

THE PARENTING ROLE AND ITS RELEVANCE TO EDUCATION

The thread running through this chapter is the connection between the role and responsibilities of parents and the remit of teachers, which extends beyond the delivery of lessons (the older, narrower, pedagogical view of teaching) to a broader-based view of educating the whole child. In this regard, and irrespective even of any school's commitment to parent participation, teachers and parents have much in common. They may well share aspirations overall for children's welfare and the maximizing, through education at school and learning at home, of their abilities and competencies. By the same token that parents, through exposure to school, become progressively informed and knowledgeable about education, it has been the fundamental premise in this chapter that it can only advantage teachers to understand more about what is involved in parenting from a theoretical standpoint as well as (for so many) from first-hand practical experience.

The key concepts selected from this chapter summarize the 'message' from the discussion: to be aware, sensitive and responsive to key features of parenting and the educational role of the family:

PARENTING STYLES

IMPORTANCE OF THE FAMILY FOR SUPPORTING CHILDREN LEARNING

SUPPORTING PARENTS

CHAPTER SUMMARY

This chapter has aimed to look critically and carefully at the key experience of being a parent. Although parenthood is one of the commonplace life experiences, it is only in recent years that it has been the subject of research enquiry. Much is being revealed about different styles of parenting, the attitudes of mothers and fathers to their role and responsibilities, and the contribution of the family overall to children's learning. Some of these themes are explored further in the next chapter.

FURTHER READING

The texts selected are ones that will cast more light on the roles of mothers, fathers and parents, and provide food for thought as to how parents can be supported and assisted in their endeavours.

Chester, L. (ed.) (1989) *Cradle and All: Women Writers on Pregnancy and Birth*. London: Faber & Faber. This is an unusual book to include in a 'professional' bibliography, but it is highly recommended. It comprises a compilation of poems, short stories and accounts of women's experiences which are illuminating, graphic, often moving depictions of the elemental experience of being mothers.

Fine, M. (ed.) (1989) *The Second Handbook on Parent Education: Contemporary Perspectives.* 2nd edition. London: Academic Press. This is a very wide-ranging text covering issues and research in parent education in the home and in school within the broader context of social policy.

Gross, J. (1989) *Psychology and Parenthood*. Milton Keynes: Open University Press. This book is a practical guide for parents and professionals, based on theoretical frameworks and explanations. It deals with a range of anxiety-provoking problems in childhood and suggests strategies for solving these.

Lewis, C. and O'Brien, M. (eds.) (1987) *Reassessing Fatherhood: New Observations on Fathers and the Modern Family*. London: Sage. This is a compilation of many perspectives on fatherhood, covering the changing role of fathers, research into fatherhood and broader societal perspectives.

REFERENCES

Ainsworth, M.D., Bell, S. and Stayton, D. (1991) Infant–mother attachment and social development: 'socialisation' as a product of reciprocal responsiveness to signals. Chapter 2 in M. Woodhead, R. Carr and P. Light (eds), *Becoming a Person*. London: Routledge and the Open University.

Ball, J. (1987) *Reactions to Motherhood*. Cambridge: Cambridge University Press.

Beail, N. and McGuire, J. (eds) (1982) *Fathers: Psychological Perspectives*. London: Junction Books.

Berk, L. (1989) *Child Development*. London: Allyn & Bacon.

Bronfenbrenner, U. (1979) *The Ecology of Human Development*. London: Harvard University Press.

Burton White, L. (1978) *The First Three Years of Life*. London: W.H. Allen.

Commission for Racial Equality (CRE) (1989) *From Cradle to School: A Practical Guide to Race Equality and Childcare*. London: CRE.

Dunn, J. (1989) The family as an educational environment in the pre-school years. In C. Desforges (ed.), *Early Childhood Education*. Edinburgh: Scottish Academic Press and the British Psychological Society.

Fine, M. (ed.) (1989) *The Second Handbook on Parent Education: Contemporary Perspectives*. London: Academic Press.

Gesell, A. and Ilg, F. (1965) *The Child from Five to Ten*. London: Hamish Hamilton.

Gross, J. (1989) *Psychology and Parenthood*. Milton Keynes: Open University Press.

Grotevant, H.D. (1989) Child development within the family context. Chapter 2 in W. Damon (ed.) *Child Development Today and Tomorrow*. London: Jossey-Bass.

Harris, P. (1986) Presenting psychological knowledge to mothers and young children. Chapter 2 in J. Harris (ed.), *Child Psychology in Action: Linking Research and Practice*. London: Croom Helm.

Health Education Council (1989) *Birth to 5: A Guide to the First Five Years of Being a Parent*. London: HEC and Harper & Row.

Kagan, J. (1979) *The Growth of the Child*. London: Methuen.

Kagan, J. (1984) *The Nature of the Child*. New York: Basic Books.

Kohner, N. (1986) *The Parent Book*. London: BBC Publications.

Lamb, M. (ed.) (1987) *The Father's Role: Cross-Cultural Perspectives*. London: Lawrence Erlbaum.

Lefrancois, G.R. (1990) *The Lifespan*. 3rd edition. Belmont, Calif.: Wadsworth.

Lewis, C. (1986) *Becoming a Father*. Milton Keynes: Open University Press.

Lewis, C. and O'Brien, M. (eds) (1987) *Reassessing Fatherhood: New Observations on Fathers and the Modern Family*. London: Sage.

McKee, L. and O'Brien, M. (eds) (1982) *The Father Figure*. London: Tavistock.

Mead, M. and Wolfenstein, M. (1970) *Childhood in Contemporary Cultures*. Chicago: University of Chicago Press.

Michaels, G.Y. and Goldberg, W. (eds) (1988) *The Transition to Parenthood*. Cambridge: Cambridge University Press.

Phoenix, A., Woollett, A. and Lloyd, E. (eds) (1991) *Motherhood: Meanings, Practices, and Ideologies*. London: Sage.

Polansky, N., Chalmers, M.A., Buttenwieser, E. and Williams, D. (1981) *Damaged Parents: An Anatomy of Child Neglect*. Chicago: University of Chicago Press.

Powell, D. (ed.) (1988) *Parent Education as Early Childhood Intervention: Emerging Directions in Theory, Research and Practice*. Norwood, NJ: Ablex.

Procaccini, J. and Kiefaber, M. (1983) *Parent Burnout*. New York: Doubleday.

Pugh, G. and De'Ath, E. (1984) *The Needs of Parents: Practice and Policy in Parent Education*. Basingstoke: Macmillan Education.

Pugh, G. and Poulton, L. (1987) *Parenting as a Job for Life*. London: National Children's Bureau.

Rutter, M. and Madge, N. (1976) *Cycles of Disadvantage*. London: Heinemann.

Shaffer, D. (1989) *Developmental Psychology: Childhood and Adolescence*. 2nd edition. Monterey, Calif.: Brooks/Cole.

Sokolov, I. and Hutton, D. (1988) *The Parents Book*. Wellingborough: Thorsons.

Thomas, G. (1992) Ecological interventions. Chapter 4 in S. Wolfendale, T. Bryans, M. Fox, A. Labram and A. Sigston (eds), *The Profession and Practice of Educational Psychology: Future Directions*. London: Cassell.

Tizard, B. (1986) *The Care of Young Children: Implications of Recent Research*. London: Thomas Coram Research Unit.

Tizard, B. and Hughes, M. (1984) *Young Children Learning*. London: Fontana.

Tucker, N. (1977) *What Is a Child?* London: Fontana.

Vetere, A. and Gale, A. (1987) *Ecological Studies of Family Life.* Chichester: Wiley.

Whitfield, R. (1980) *Education for Family Life: Some New Policies for Child Care.* London: Hodder & Stoughton.

Wolfendale, S. (1983) *Parental Participation in Children's Development and Education.* London: Gordon & Breach.

Wolfendale, S. (1992) *Primary Schools and Special Needs: Policy, Planning and Provision.* 2nd edition. London: Cassell.

Woolfson, R. (1989) *Understanding your Child: A Parents' Guide to Child Psychology.* London: Faber & Faber.

Yapp, N. (1991) *My Problem Child: Practical Strategies for Understanding, Helping, and Coping with your Problem Child.* Harmondsworth: Penguin.

Addresses

Commission for Racial Equality (CRE), Elliot House, 10–12 Allington Street, London SW1E 5EH.

Thomas Coram Research Unit, 41 Brunswick Square, London WC1N 1AZ.

CHAPTER 4

The home as an environment for learning

CHAPTER OVERVIEW

This chapter expands on various themes, identified in the previous chapter, to do with parents' role in children's learning and the educational role of the family in general. Specifically, the significant developments in parental involvement in reading over the last few years are described, as are other related initiatives in the areas of numeracy, literacy, language, other curriculum areas and working with parents to manage behaviour in the home. Finally, the contribution of parents to children's learning, development and overall progress in terms of their experience and skills is examined.

THE INFLUENCE OF THE HOME AS A PLACE FOR LEARNING

It needs to be stressed at the outset that learning in the home is perceived to be complementary to school-based learning, or indeed to learning wherever it takes place. 'Learning' is taken as gaining information, finding out, acquiring concepts, making connections, gaining specific skills and solving problems. Learning can be formal and intentional, as in school or via a specific home-based programme, or informal and incidental, occurring for all of us all of the time, wherever we happen to be.

In fact, children's learning is a mix of intentional and incidental. The rationale behind so many of the home-based learning projects is that they capitalize on the existing, mostly incidental learning that occurs at home and in the family context, and also maximizes the skills that parents exercise already in teaching and training their children.

PARENTS AS EDUCATORS

Research cited in the previous chapter (see references in Chapter 3 to Tizard, 1986; Dunn, 1989) has established how family interaction and milieu play a significant part in children's acquisition of language, concepts and social processes. Goode (1987) cites Wells's research into language acquisition, and points out that conversations at home arise naturally and spontaneously from an activity in hand or a natural interaction with a family member. From these observations, Goode goes on to analyse the nature of learning at home, and offers a typology of 'Parents as Educators' (p. 118) with a threefold categorization – confirmatory, complementary, compensatory – and descriptors within each category.

In a wide-ranging review of contemporary work, Topping (1986) notes the current trend:

> Instead of working to make parents pale mechanistic shadows of teachers, operating some transplanted fragment of 'professional' technique, modern projects focus much more on the unique contribution of parents to the development of their children – enhancing the naturalistic skills of parents and taking their views and priorities very much into account. (p. 4)

In describing the findings from a major project lasting a number of years, Athey (1990) summarizes how the professional–parent partnership in learning was forged and how children's learning was enhanced as a consequence. Two of her conclusions are especially pertinent in the context of this chapter:

- 'the parents had no difficulty in broadening their concept of parenthood to include knowledge of their children's cognitive functioning as this functioning became illuminated during the project'. (p. 207)

- 'Teachers of young children could make a revolutionary move forward in developing a pedagogy of the early years if they recorded how they have conceptualised and shared their professional concepts with parents together with subsequent gains made by children'. (p. 206)

A number of other writers and practitioners assert their complete faith, based on tried and proven methods, in parents' ability and competence in 'teaching' children; not, as Topping emphasizes, in ways that 'ape' teachers but in their own unique and distinctive ways, drawing upon the best natural resource: their relationship with their children (Taylor, 1984; Griffiths and Hamilton, 1987; Sullivan, 1988). Indeed, the Home and School Council has published a whole series of pamphlets based on these premises and covering a range of subjects for parents and children to work on together (see address at end of chapter).

Macbeth (1989) sees home-based learning as a corollary to school-based learning, within a compact or alliance characterized as a 'mutual information exchange' (p. 69). This conveys the reciprocity which is a characteristic of partnership (Wolfendale, 1983; and see Chapter 2). But Macbeth also states that the area of home-based learning is 'an under-researched and probably under-estimated facet of the child's educational experience' (p. 73). He is certainly justified in this assertion in terms of 'pure' research, but there is a wealth of information from many applied projects in many parts of the world that not only attest to the effectiveness of home-based learning but highlight the aspects that work (see reference, too, to *Portage* in Chapter 7). We will examine several of these areas in the next sections.

PARENTAL INVOLVEMENT IN READING

One or two seminal projects in the late 1970s (see Hewison, 1985) provided the inspiration and models for a plethora of subsequent initiatives. Topping and Wolfendale (1985) describe the various methods employed and the outcomes of many of these ventures, and outline a series of procedures involved in setting up, monitoring and evaluating home- and school-based shared teaching activities.

Overall, the 'movement' known as 'parental involvement in children's reading' has generated unique technologies and methodologies, and a number of features common to many such initiatives can be identified.

Common threads for home-based reading

Agreement between teacher and parent; reading activity at home, nightly, or several times a week; limit of 10–15 minutes per session; some training in the chosen method; use of a record card, passing between parent(s) and teacher.

Techniques

Parent listening; paired reading; turn taking; pause, prompt and praise (parents as tutors); precision teaching; direct instruction. (See Topping and Wolfendale, 1985, for a description of these techniques; also Morgan, 1986, on paired reading.)

Planning considerations

Usually the projects conform to some kind of sequence that encompasses these elements:

- starting points (existing policy and practice on teaching reading and involving parents in school);
- planning (objectives, materials, assessment, record-keeping, time-scale);
- action (preparing children and parents, training, setting up the projects);
- maintaining and monitoring (checking on practicalities, record-keeping, meetings, including home visits, assessment);
- measurement and evaluation (assessment, feedback from participants, reviewing progress, planning future action).

(See Chapter 32 in Topping and Wolfendale, 1985, for a comprehensive planning outline.)

Summary of ways in which parents are involved

Home-based ways are:

- shared reading: turn taking; paired reading; pause, prompt and praise (parents as tutors);
- fostering language, conversation, discussion, sharing experiences.

Parents in school (the mirror image of home-based learning) act as 'co-workers': hearing children read; reading stories to children.

Descriptions of a number of schemes are contained in several books which have been written for parents and teachers following the running of successful schemes (Griffiths and Hamilton, 1984; Young and Tyre, 1985; Branston and Provis, 1986; Bloom, 1987; Davis and Stubbs, 1988). To some extent, these are intended as 'how to' books; see also Body (1989, 1990).

Outcomes of parental involvement in reading schemes

In many school–home ventures, the criterion of success has been whether or not children's reading scores have been significantly improved as a probable result of their parents having shared reading activities with them at home. Pre- and post-test measures do provide an index of change, but it is difficult to ascribe positive changes conclusively to parental input. It is not easy, for example, to determine whether increase in attainment is due to quantitative aspects (that is, having more adults acting as teachers and role models) and/or qualitative ones (that is, parental tutoring skills having a direct effect on children's performance).

Another issue in determining effectiveness is whether or not there is a 'best buy' technique, demonstrably superior to others. Paired reading has its ardent adherents (Morgan, 1986; Topping, 1989), but there are those who champion the view that it is less the teaching technique than the setting conditions that are crucial to successful outcomes. Drummond and colleagues provided a 'menu' of choice of techniques in their initiative (Drummond, 1990).

Another way of gauging the effectiveness of schemes is to sample the views of participants; that is, parents, children, teachers (see Topping and Wolfendale, 1985). Some researchers have observed parents and children 'at work' together and recorded the various skills of parents as tutors in:

- encouraging (prompting) a reading response;
- responding to error and application of error-correcting techniques;
- use of picture cues or other contextual clues;
- giving the child enough time to self-correct;
- use of specific techniques (such as paired reading).

Monitoring of parent teaching effectiveness is another evaluative approach (see the self-report form in Gillett and Bernard, 1989, pp. 86–7). In another Australian project, Kemp (1989) and colleagues regard training of parents as a prerequisite; increasing fluency with new-found skills can then be monitored as a key part of the operation of a project.

Conclusions from surveys and reviews

Raban and Geekie (1989) review a range of parental involvement in reading programmes and discuss the sometimes equivocal nature of the cited gains. They conclude, as does Toomey (1992) in his wide-ranging review of methods and outcomes, that there are a number of variables that need to be researched before we can definitely ascribe criteria for success, although reviewers seem to agree that generally this is an effective area of home–school participation (Topping, 1991).

A considerable amount of attention has been given to parental involvement in reading as a case study in this chapter, since this is a seminal area that has influenced other curriculum areas in terms of techniques and methodologies. We continue with a look at some of these other areas.

PARENTAL INVOLVEMENT IN NUMERACY

The area of parental involvement in numeracy began to develop in part as a consequence of the influence of home-based reading schemes; but quickly developed as a valid area in its own right and of equal status. Although many schools have, over the years, embarked upon their own attempts (necessarily modest) to link school-based number work with similar work at home, particularly at primary level, it has been the larger-scale projects that have inevitably become well known.

Bamford and Arora (1988) report upon the effectiveness of a project that has already spanned seven or eight years and included infant and junior schools, parents and children in programmes consisting of games, puzzles and paired maths activities. A scheme that has had considerable take-up in many parts of the country is IMPACT (Maths for Parents and Children and Teachers Project: Merttens and Vass, 1990), which makes numeracy skill acquisition enjoyable and firmly roots most of the activities within routine domestic events and circumstances. (This is in fact how we learn many of the key concepts of counting, sorting, measuring and weighing.) For parents wanting reference books on these activities, there are detailed paperbacks by Liebeck (1984) and Graham (1985).

Perhaps we can be confident in predicting that this is a growth area, as parents seek to help their children with a National Curriculum core subject.

PARENTAL INVOLVEMENT IN LITERACY

The emphasis of earlier work in the areas of reading and, to a lesser extent, number and parental involvement has been on measurable skill acquisition at later stages. There is some evidence now that the perspective is broadening to encompass both the acquisition of a range of literacy skills, and also adults, whether teachers or parents or both, helping equip children for *life-long literacy*.

Within the definitions of literacy given by Whitehead (1990) and Wray and Medwell (1991), a number of activities characteristic of 'literate behaviour' can be listed, in order to demonstrate how teachers and parents could agree a common agenda for working co-operatively towards not only functional literacy (for the given purposes in school, at home and in the community), but also life-long literacy. In school and home settings there is a common desire for children to develop competence in:

- reading for pleasure and information;
- using the printed word to understand and make sense of the world;
- using a range of media;
- questioning, weighing arguments, appraising evidence, being critical;
- responding to written requests, completing forms, comprehending signs and instructions in public places;
- using language competently in all its rich and varied ways.

As far as parents' contribution to the acquisition of these skills is concerned, research and observation confirms that they offer the following *specific skills* (for example, as reading tutors):

- skill in using methods (based on some training);
- use of feedback and correction techniques (again, based on training);
- provision of 'stimulus material' in the home (books, other resources).

But parents as educators bring a lot more to the enterprise, including *general skills* such as:

- knowledge of their child – predicting and understanding behaviour;
- life experience and knowledge; accumulating wisdom and perspective; passing on these insights;
- being decision-makers and arbiters (for example, their socializing role);
- offering love, security, reassurance and validation of the child ('teaching' within a caring context).

Compare these lists with the parenting functions set out in Chapter 2 and look for complementarity.

Developing life-long literacy: focus on involving parents in language development

Communication and verbal discourse are the main currencies in human interaction, so it is not surprising that a number of workers in the parental involvement field see language-based work as a fundamental prerequisite to developing life-long literacy in all its manifestations. Earlier reference has been made to this in the current chapter as well as in Chapter 3.

The home is a rich and fruitful context for 'natural' discourse to take place, as has been said, and the programmes that have been developed and tried out aim to complement the communication that already takes place with specified activities designed to foster particular aspects of language. For example, in WORD PLAY (Wolfendale and Bryans, 1986) the intention is to provide parents with a range of language activities, word games and story and drama exercises which can arise spontaneously or which can be carried out during a short session daily or several times a week. In another project, Weinberger *et al*. (1990) describe ways of working with parents – at home as well as in schools or centres – to promote children's early literacy development through experience of environmental print, early writing and sharing books. The rationale for this Sheffield-based project is that knowledge of literacy at school entry is a strong predictor of later attainment, so clearly home environment and parents have a key role to play. The authors refer to the pre-school stage of emerging literacy as the 'roots' of literacy. (See also the case studies in Chapters 10 and 11 by Lynda Pearce and Ray Phillips for descriptions of literacy-based parental involvement projects.)

Finally, the importance of this area in its own right and as a precursor to related literacy skills is summed up by two writers urging parents to listen as well as talk to their children (Crystal, 1986; Wiener, 1988). These sentiments are in accord with contemporary concerns over reading standards (Turner, 1991). As Topping (1991) has asserted, and as has been borne out by a House of Commons Select Committee looking into reading standards and the teaching of reading during 1991, we must continue to capitalize on the rich resources we have in parents as partners and educators.

It might be helpful at this point to engage in a reflective exercise about some of these concepts and initiatives.

EXERCISE: Thinking about parents as educators

Purpose: To consider the desirability, accuracy and efficacy of the term.

What to do: Reflect on the examples given in this chapter of parents acting as educators (tutors is another term) and consider these questions:

* Does the description 'parents as educators' adequately convey what parents do?
* Is it a limiting description?
* Does it sound like a copy of what teachers do?
* Does it fairly reflect everything that parents do?
* Can you suggest an alternative description?

Comments: These questions are designed to stimulate discussion, and you may well think of others you can add and discuss. Although there are no 'answers', it is hoped that this exercise will clarify thinking and attitudes on this topic.

We turn now to broader aspects of the home as a setting where children's learning takes place and in which parents are not only educators but agents to facilitate behaviour change. It is arguable whether or not this area of discussion rightly belongs to the (later) chapter examining parental involvement and special needs, since behaviour problems can be conceptualized along the dimensions of 'need' and difficulty. In reality the demarcation lines are blurred, for there are few parents (and teachers?) who do not at some time in their parenting careers experience concern, anxiety and stress over their children's behaviour and adjustment, with concomitant doubts as to the effectiveness of their chosen strategy for solving the problems of the moment. So the issues, whether they appear minor or major at the time, are familiar to most of us, and the examination of the part that parents play in behaviour change would seem to be a legitimate part of a chapter on the influence of the home environment on learning and behaviour.

The stance taken, then, is similar to that of Frude (1991) in asserting that a range of these problems are ones commonly faced by families. This is compatible with a view that perceives the importance of assisting and supporting parents and other family members to rear their young effectively (Rapoport, 1987).

THE PARENTAL ROLE IN THE MANAGEMENT OF BEHAVIOUR

Several books that aim to support parents and suggest strategies were mentioned in the previous chapter, and a number of others outline quite detailed approaches, if not programmes, to bring about behaviour change in children. These are based on theoretical principles: for example, behavioural approaches (Westmacott and Cameron, 1981; Herbert, 1985). Although untargeted in that they are aimed at any and all parents, the ideas and solutions contained in these books can become targeted via a programme drawn up by parents, with or without professional help. Some of the suggestions undoubtedly validate strategies parents have already tried, with or without success; others, however, are based on research and intervention studies and have demonstrated their effectiveness. These books exemplify the potential of the parent–professional partnership in behaviour change (parent and teacher, parent and educational psychologist, for example), whereby parental commitment and insights combine with professional training and cumulative experience of similar situations.

As is pointed out by Wolfendale (1990), there is a long history of such collaboration between parents and workers in child guidance clinics and school (now invariably called educational) psychological services, though by definition these behaviour change programmes have had a problem focus (Schaefer and Briesmeister, 1989). Recent calls have come (Elton Report, 1989; Wolfendale and Bryans, 1989) for broadening and extending parental participation in behaviour management in school as well as at home, the rationale being:

- that such inclusion is compatible with increased parental involvement in education generally;
- that consultation with and involvement of parents in discussion and planning of school policy on discipline and behaviour management constitute preventive measures of a positive nature;

- that parents have complementary skills and 'equivalent expertise' to contribute (Wolfendale, 1983).

Not only did the Elton Report (1989) recommend that there be increased parental involvement in agreeing, implementing and reviewing discipline and behaviour management school policies, but so too have educational psychologists. As has been said, educational psychologists have traditionally played a key role both in schools and with families in this area. In a publication devoted to the relevance of the Elton Report to educational psychology practice (Fox *et al.*, 1991), a specific suggestion is made for: 'development of consultancy models, involving groups of parents in the school community, incorporating parental perspectives in whole school policies in the definition of procedures. This would help parents to encourage good behaviour and to back up school strategies' (p. 17). For further ideas and suggestions (additional to references cited above) see Herbert (1981), Hinton (1989), Galvin *et al.* (1991).

SUPPORTING THE FAMILY: A COMMUNITY RESPONSIBILITY?

To this point, there has been an implicit supposition that responsibility is shared only by those collaborating on a given project to effect children's learning and behaviour change. There is of course a wider canvas, such as a school's collective involvement or policy on working with parents (explored further in later chapters), and, broader still, the community nexus.

Community education has had a twenty- to twenty-five-year history in Britain, with many initiatives mirroring the American Head Start and Follow Through experiences (see Chapter 2 and the relevant references; also Wolfendale, 1983, Chapter 5; Rennie, 1985). Models of parental involvement and support in such initiatives which link home, school and the broader community have been various; they range from bureaucrat-initiated and -dominated projects, in which financial control is not necessarily held by the participants (some government grant projects exemplify this top-down model); to 'street level', community-inspired ventures which have managed to raise money from a variety of sources and which, as a consequence of having generated the original ideas and expressed the need, retain some control over decisions and expenditure. See the case study by Ray Phillips in Chapter 10, and Phillips (1989).

Each model is partly defined by its (apparent) attitudes towards parents. We could conceptualize a continuum ranging from a patronizing attitude that parents are in need of support and guidance from 'experts' to an empowerment-focused attitude (see Chapter 2), epitomized by the central tenet that, with the appropriate resources, parents from all kinds of social and educational backgrounds can develop and maximize their competencies and potential as parents, solve or cope with their problems and be self-reliant.

The concept of collective responsibility for family well-being is at heart a political issue, and the ideology of the political party in government at any one time is reflected in social policy and legislation. The associated issues of financial support for various kinds of family unit and day care for young children continue to exercise professionals and parents alike. A major piece of legislation covering England and Wales which took effect in October 1991, the 1989 Children Act, does reflect the contemporary view that society in the form of the state has certain responsibilities towards enabling and supporting parents in their task of child-rearing. Certainly its philosophy endorses 'parents as partners', and its provisions set out duties for local authorities to provide a range and level of services for young children, particularly those defined by the Act as being 'in need', in which family and parental involvement are paramount. Parental responsibility and the rights that flow from that responsibility are made explicit, as are the commensurate responsibilities for professional (and voluntary) services to support parents and carers in carrying out these responsibilities fully (HMSO, 1991).

Some of the ramifications of this legislation are more appropriately explored in Chapter 7, but it is relevant here to identify the rather blurred distinction between family- and child-focused intervention (directed at children deemed to have special needs, have disabilities or be socially disadvantaged) and family support (aimed at all children, on the premise that child-rearing *should* be a corporate responsibility). The whole area of intervention is conceptually complex, as was touched upon above when a continuum of attitudes towards parents was postulated. Zigler (1990) sketches the history of American child- and family-focused intervention and how various phases, each reflecting contemporary thinking and practice, have characterized the whole movement.

As Meisels and Shonkoff (1990) outline, the deficit model (giving rise to the term 'compensatory intervention'), whereby the child received appropriate stimulation to compensate for alleged social, intellectual and environmental deprivation, gave way to a broader view which perceived the child as part of a viable, vibrant, dynamic family unit that was socially valid (even if economically deprived). So programmes incorporated family dimensions into educationally based intervention, which in turn gave way to interventions that emphasized the legitimate contribution of parents to children's development and learning – the parents as educators model, in part. As Zigler (1990) spells out, these paradigms included ecological perspectives (see Chapter 3) and the family systems approach.

Integral, then, to the notion of *collective responsibility* nowadays

47

is the acknowledged primacy of parents in children's lives and as influences upon their development, along with a view (not always backed up with resources, however) that society, through state and community and mediated by professional workers, is also accountable in providing for children's welfare through supporting parents. This stance is evidenced in the emphasis on multidisciplinary co-operation in the 1989 Children Act (HMSO, 1991) (see too the discussion by Harbin and McNulty, 1990, on these issues, and in the context of similar American legislation).

To summarize this section: while we may conclude that there is plenty of evidence to show that parents as 'educators' are involved in a whole range of home-based learning and behavioural programmes, there are diverse views as to whether or not such intervention is 'remedial' or preventive. One way – perhaps ultimately the most constructive – to deal with such a conceptually complex area is to take an equal opportunities perspective, which asserts that all children and their parents/carers should have the right to access to opportunities to participate in such projects on the fundamental premise of *entitlement*. We can target differentially, on the same principle as that of curriculum differentiation, according to criteria identified to suit each family, and acknowledging that not all families will want or be able to take up such opportunities at any one time. But if the provision is available to all, we do not need to characterize or label programmes invidiously ('remedial', etc., as referred to above).

ASSESSING PARENTAL SKILLS

The final part of this chapter attempts to summarize a range of skills that parents bring to home- and family-based initiatives. Some of these were described earlier in fairly formal résumés based on results and findings from many of the projects. I will now present, as an illuminative counterpoint to these lists, some responses to exercises carried out as part of in-service workshops for parents and professionals over several years.

The initial request to workshop participants is simple: 'Under the heading *What do we have to offer?*, in small groups please discuss what skills and experience parents bring to joint ventures with professionals (teachers, educational psychologists, social workers, health visitors, and so on).' The instruction continues: 'List skills derived from life experience; from training if applicable; from facts and knowledge; from the use of techniques and approaches.' Participants were then asked to identify their future training and support needs which, if met, would facilitate effective, co-operative working with one another.

Verbatim responses are presented below from two workshops out of more than thirty conducted over several years. The first took place at an annual conference of the Welsh Preschool Playgroups Association, where all the participants were parents and some had professional qualifications and experience:

EXISTING EXPERTISE
Experience: as parent (all); as teacher (some); as nurse (some); as playgroup leader (all); of children (all); of fostering (some); of own childhood (all); life experience (all); using past to predict future (all); use of common sense (all); of work with special needs (some).
Knowledge: PPA courses (all); teacher training (some); of local resources (some); of family life and children (all); of child development (all); of referral procedure (some); of 1981 Education Act (some); of local community (all).
Skills/techniques: play group courses (all); teaching (some); child development courses (all); natural sympathy (all); leadership (some); use of materials and toys (all); child management (all); observation (all); household and craft skills (all); first aid (some).

We can see that the mixture comprises a number of bedrock universal experiences, with some selective experiences and skills.

This sharing experience provided the basis for the next part of the exercise. Clearly the needs identified do not apply to every participant:

Knowledge: of local resources; of school systems; curriculum; examinations; career guidance; of dealing with systems; of confidence to negotiate with professionals; confidence in being a parent.
Skills/techniques: child management; at relationships; at being a friend to my children; self-appraisal and making objective assessment of a child; passing on life-knowledge; communication; being a resource and support; helping children's early learning.
Specific courses: child development; baby and childcare; language; sign language; knowledge of reading, writing, maths, computers; Portage; counselling; nutrition, health; birth control; parents' groups; training professionals to deal with parents.
    Perceived training and support needs include specific knowledge, training in techniques and approaches and means by which to become empowered and confident to 'work the systems'.

The second set of responses comes from a workshop for teachers, most of whom brought professional and parental perspectives. Six groups generated lists, one of which is given here:

PRESENT LEVEL
Experience: child development; commitment; stress; caring for a child; parental affinity with child; learning from experience of child rearing; life experience.
Knowledge: dealing with officialdom; self-help; self-knowledge; co-counselling; professional education; stimulation appropriate for child.
Skills: understanding behaviour; helping a child; teaching; crafts; management; advising people.

FUTURE NEEDS
Knowledge: care schemes; how to talk to and exist with others; calm approach to child; how to maintain a positive attitude; paired reading; parental involvement in schools.

Skills: Portage; playing with your child; music with your child; communicating with the handicapped; teaching reading; patience; teaching my child in a structured way; develop inner confidence to match outer display.

This list, like the previous one, represents a mixture of specific and general skills areas in which the participants felt they needed further training and support in order to work more effectively.

The key concepts selected epitomize the main features of many home-based learning initiatives:

HOME AS A LEARNING ENVIRONMENT	**PARENTS AS EDUCATORS**
EQUIVALENT EXPERTISE	**COLLECTIVE RESPONSIBILITY**

CHAPTER SUMMARY

This chapter has roved widely over the landscape of *parents as educators*, focusing particularly on home-based learning and behaviour management initiatives, within the broader context of society's obligations and responsibility to support families in the task of child-rearing. Finally, to complement the more formal presentation of parental skills, the findings of skills-listing workshops have been presented in the participants' (parents and professionals) own words.

FURTHER READING

The four texts that have been selected for further reading encompass the gamut of home-based initiatives from various perspectives; for example, Meisels and Shonkoff for academic research and social policy, Topping for a wide-ranging review of parents-as-educators projects, Topping and Wolfendale for first-hand accounts of many of the parental-involvement-in-reading schemes, and Herbert for a compendium of practical advice for parents, placed within clearly articulated theoretical frameworks.

Herbert, M. (1985) *Caring for your Children: A Practical Guide.* Harmondsworth: Penguin.

Meisels, S. and Shonkoff, J. (eds) (1990) *Handbook of Early Childhood Intervention.* Cambridge: Cambridge University Press.

Topping, K. and Wolfendale, S. (eds) (1985) *Parental Involvement in Children's Reading.* London: Croom Helm.

Topping, K. (1986) *Parents as Educators.* London: Croom Helm.

REFERENCES

Athey, C. (1990) *Extending Thought in Young Children: A Parent-Teacher Partnership*. London: Paul Chapman.

Bamford, J. and Arora, T. (1988) MATHS – Multiply Attainments Through Home Support: progress and development. *Educational and Child Psychology*, Vol. 5, No. 4, pp. 48–54.

Bloom, W. (1987) *Partnership with Parents in Reading*. London: Hodder & Stoughton.

Body, W. (1989) *Learning to Read and Write*. Harlow: Longman.

Body, W. (ed.) (1990) *Help your Child with Reading*. London: BBC.

Branston, P. and Provis, M. (1986) *Children and Parents Enjoy Reading*. London: Hodder & Stoughton.

Crystal, D. (1986) *Listen to your Child*. Harmondsworth: Penguin.

Davis, C. and Stubbs, R. (1988) *Shared Reading in Practice*. Milton Keynes: Open University Press.

Drummond, A., Godfrey, L. and Sattin, R. (1990) Promoting parental involvement in reading. *Support for Learning*, Vol. 5, No. 3, pp. 141–6.

Elton Report (1989) *Discipline in Schools: Report of the Committee of Enquiry, chaired by Lord Elton*. London: HMSO.

Fox, M., Hayes, S. and Wolfendale, S. (eds) (1991) *Managing Behaviour: Implications for Educational Psychologists of the Elton Report*. Available from Psychology Department, University of East London.

Frude, N. (1991) *Understanding Family Problems: A Psychological Approach*. Chichester: Wiley.

Galvin, P., Mercer, S. and Costa, P. (1991) *Building a Better Behaved School*. Harlow: Longman.

Gillett, S. and Bernard, M. (1989) *Reading Rescue – A Parents' Guide*. 2nd edition. Victoria: Australian Council for Educational Research.

Goode, J. (1987) Parents as educators. In J. Bastiani (ed.), *Parents and Teachers*. Vol. 1. *Perspectives on Home–School Relations*. Windsor: NFER-Nelson.

Graham, A. (1985) *Help your Child with Maths*. London: Fontana.

Griffiths, A. and Hamilton, D. (1984) *Parent, Teacher, Child*. London: Methuen.

Griffiths, A. and Hamilton, D. (1987) *Learning at Home*. London: Methuen.

Harbin, G. and McNulty, B.C. (1990) Policy implementation: perspectives on service coordination and interagency cooperations. Chapter 3 in S. Meisels and J. Shonkoff (eds) *Handbook of Early Childhood Intervention*. Cambridge: Cambridge University Press.

Herbert, M. (1981) *Behavioural Treatment of Problem Children: A Practice Manual*. London: Academic Press.

Herbert, M. (1985) *Caring for your Children: A Practical Guide*. Harmondsworth: Penguin.

Hewison, J. (1985) Parental involvement and reading attainments. Implications of research. Chapter 4 in K. Topping and S. Wolfendale (eds), *Parental Involvement in Children's Reading*. London: Croom Helm.

Hinton, S. (1990) *The ABC of Behaviour: A Parents' Handbook*. Ewell: Media Resources, Surrey County Council.

HMSO (1991) *The Children Act 1989: Guidance and Regulations*. Vol. 2. *Family Support, Day Care and Educational Provision for Young Children*. London: HMSO.

Kemp, M. (1989) Parents as tutors: a case study of a special education programme in oral reading. Unpublished doctoral thesis. University of Queensland.

Liebeck, P. (1984) *How Children Learn Mathematics: A Guide for Parents and Teachers*. Harmondsworth: Penguin.

Macbeth, A. (1989) *Involving Parents: Effective Parent–Teacher Relations*. Oxford: Heinemann Educational.

Meisels, S. and Shonkoff, J. (eds) (1990) *Handbook of Early Childhood Intervention*. Cambridge: Cambridge University Press.

Merttens, R. and Vass, J. (1990) *Bringing School Home: Children and Parents Learning Together*. London: Hodder & Stoughton.

Morgan, R. (1986) *Helping Children Read*. London: Methuen.

Phillips, R. (1989) The Newham Parents' Centre: a study of parent involvement as a community action contribution to inner city community development. Chapter 7 in S. Wolfendale (ed.), *Parental Involvement: Developing Networks between School, Home and Community*. London: Cassell.

Raban, B. and Geekie, P. (1989) Reading research in Great Britain, 1987. *Reading*, Vol. 23, No. 3, pp. 133–49.

Rapoport, R. (1987) *New Interventions for Children and Youth*. Cambridge: Cambridge University Press.

Rennie, J. (ed.) (1985) *British Community Primary Schools*. Lewes: Falmer.

Schaefer, C. and Briesmeister, J. (eds) (1989) *Handbook of Parent Training: Parents as Co-therapists for Children's Behaviour Problems*. Chichester: Wiley.

Sullivan, M. (1988) *Parents and Schools*. Leamington Spa: Scholastic Publications.

Taylor, G. (1984) *Be your Child's Natural Teacher*. London: Impact Books.

Toomey, D. (1992) An examination of some UK, USA and Australasian studies of parents and children's literacy development: lessons for school practice. Contact at Centre for the Study of Community, Education and Social Change, La Trobe University, Bundoora, Victoria 3083, Australia.

Topping, K. (1986) *Parents as Educators*. London: Croom Helm.

Topping, K. (1991) Achieving more with less: raising reading standards via parental involvement and peer tutoring. *Support for Learning*, Vol. 6, No. 3, pp. 112–16.

Topping, K. and Wolfendale, S. (eds) (1985) *Parental Involvement in Children's Reading*. London: Croom Helm.

Turner, M. (1991) Finding out. *Support for Learning*, Vol. 6, No. 3, pp. 99–1031.

Weinberger, J., Hannon, P. and Nutbrown, C. (1990) *Ways of Working with Parents to Promote Early Literacy Development*. Sheffield: University of Sheffield, Division of Education.

Westmacott, S. and Cameron, R.J. (1981) *Behaviour Can Change*. Basingstoke: Globe Education.

Whitehead, M. (1990) *Language and Literacy in the Early Years*. London: Paul Chapman.

Wiener, H. (1988) *Talk with your Child: Using Conversation to Enhance Language Development*. Harmondsworth: Penguin.

Wolfendale, S. (1983) *Parental Participation in Children's Development and Education*. London: Gordon & Breach.

Wolfendale, S. (1990) Involving parents in behaviour management – a whole-school approach. Chapter 15 in M. Scherer, I. Gersch and L. Fry (eds), *Meeting Disruptive Behaviour: Assessment, Intervention and Partnership*. Basingstoke: Macmillan.

Wolfendale, S. and Bryans, T. (1986) *WORD PLAY: Language Activities for Young Children and their Parents*. Stafford: National Association for Remedial Education (now NASEN; National Association for Special Educational Needs).

Wolfendale, S. and Bryans, T. (1989) *Managing Behaviour: A Practical Framework for Schools*. Stafford: National Association for Remedial Education (now NASEN; National Association for Special Educational Needs).

Wray, D. and Medwell, J. (1991) *Literacy and Language in the Primary Years*. London: Routledge.

Young, P. and Tyre, C. (1985) *Teach your Children to Read*. London: Fontana/Collins.

Zigler, E. (1990) Foreword to S. Meisels and J. Shonkoff (eds), *Handbook of Early Childhood Intervention*. Cambridge: Cambridge University Press.

ADDRESSES

Home and School Council, 81 Rustlings Road, Sheffield S11 7AB.
Media Resources, Surrey County Council, Glyn House, Ewell, Surrey.

CHAPTER 5

Parents in school

This chapter is a kind of mirror image of the previous one, in that it portrays a number of the many activities which denote parental involvement in schools. It takes essentially a school focus, whereas Chapter 4 presented parents as educators within the home. Having given several major areas of within-school parental involvement, the chapter then offers some summarizing comments.

PRESENTING THE EVIDENCE

Chapter 2 traced the advent of parents in schools and provided an introductory review of the whole field. In this chapter, several of the main initiatives that were trailed there will be examined in more detail. These initiatives represent what has become the mainstream of parental involvement, which is now routine practice in many schools, though, as surveys confirm, take-up across Britain is still far from uniform, and standard practice in some areas is emerging practice in others. The evidence of current practice in this chapter is backed up and consolidated by the case studies in Chapters 10 and 11, which epitomize in even more detail the solid base from which the initiatives described emanate.

Also in Chapter 2, the possible effects and implications of the Education Reform Act upon home–school links and parent–teacher relations were mentioned, but not pursued. In this chapter, ERA will hardly loom, for the work described had its origins and gestations mostly in the 1980s. Chapters 8 and 9 directly take up the issues arising from recent legislation and consider the match between legal provisions and emerging initiatives in home–school links. So those chapters will deal with the 'state of the art' in parental involvement.

There has been a steady flow of texts over the last ten years or so documenting parental involvement initiatives. Overview texts include Wolfendale (1983, 1989), Cullingford (1985), Bastiani (1987, 1988), Macbeth (1989) and Macleod (1989), each of which will be quoted from in this chapter. First-hand and graphic accounts come from Grant (1989) and Stacey (1991). Survey evidence has been less forthcoming, but a helpful data-base is provided by HMI (1991a), and Jowett *et al.* (1991).

So what do parents do in school?

First, as a cue, check back to Chapter 2 for the initial list summarizing the major areas of involvement over recent years. Below are listed some of the areas that Sallis (1989) considers are 'good practice today':

- accessible and welcoming school buildings;
- a place for parents in school (parents' room, some earmarked space);
- school–home reading scheme;
- written and verbal communication;
- parents helping in classrooms and with the curriculum.

Sallis readily acknowledges that this list is a bald résumé. Other summaries include the Wheel of Parental Involvement (Wolfendale, 1992), which segments the many activities subsumed generally under 'parents in schools'. Galvin *et al.* (1991) presents a long checklist of such activities under these headings: support in non-educational school activities; information giving and social links; parents' involvement in their own child's education; school education processes; school management and policy making.

The NFER survey (Jowett *et al.*, 1991) confirmed the prevalence (but again, remember the reported wide range and patchiness of provision) of parents in school activities: parents as governors (all schools, required by statute); involvement of parents in their children's reading (see Chapter 4 as well as later in this chapter); involvement of parents in other curriculum areas (mostly maths, but computer work, dance and home economics were also reported); and general involvement in schools (covering classes for parents in school, such as English as a Second Language; practical assistance by parents, such as painting school buildings; parents giving talks or running after-school leisure clubs for pupils; parent–teacher meetings to explain the curriculum, other aspects of school functioning and school plans; and, for many schools, the traditional parent–teacher association as a forum for joint activity).

The HMI survey carried out during 1989–90 (HMI, 1991a), in contrast, focused on thirty-two primary and thirty-eight secondary schools, each of which was visited for one day. The visit comprised discussions, observations and collection of documentation. Differences between primary and secondary schools in the area of parental involvement are significant, and these are explored later in this chapter. In general, though, the HMI survey confirms the increasing presence of parents in schools, and not only a growing commitment of schools to pursuing joint activities such as the ones listed above, but also their responsiveness to the new requirement to report children's progress to their parents (explored further in Chapter 6). HMI report that 'in all but two of the primary schools parents helped in classrooms though, as a percentage of the whole parent population of each school, the proportion involved in this way was small' (p. 8).

Likewise, the HMI survey drew attention to the fact that 'not all the work involving parents was profitable' (p. 9) and this observation is a salutory reminder that lip-service to joint co-operation, even tokenistic adherence to the spirit of joint co-operation, is not sufficient. There remains much to do in terms of research and hypothesis testing to establish the clear benefits to all of such activities.

APPRAISING THE EVIDENCE

A summary paper produced by Macbeth and Munn (1990) identified four areas which require continuing research: parental influence on education; parents and teacher education; monitoring and evaluation; and an action programme.

In the appraisal of some of the areas of involvement that comprises the bulk of this chapter, we can see that evidence for effectiveness does already exist in some form or another. For example, as was noted in Chapter 4, a range of measures have been used in parental involvement in reading projects, including assessing children's reading and literacy performance and sampling participants' views. Controlled and comparative measures have been used (see Plewis *et al.*, 1990). A number of writers and researcher-participants advocate evaluation being built into projects and initiatives from the start as integral features, and 'stress the need for evaluation to relate to the original intentions and goals of those involved, to acknowledge the spirit of the enterprise and the ability to offer sympathetic, although critical, judgement' (Bastiani, 1988, p. 187).

Research and evaluation activities are not synonymous, but they need to be complementary in the case of parental involvement in education, which at any one time is dynamic, linked essentially to and part of practice – it can never be a laboratory-type situation, wherein all variables and contingencies can easily be controlled. The extent of the rigour depends on what the researchers and participants want from the enterprise. That is, a 'low level' of evidence may be the views of parents, children and teachers, which can be as valid and valuable as complicated 'higher-level' evidence such as outcome measures (for example, reading scores, evidence of changed behaviour, academic performance and so on).

Because research findings and evaluation data pave the way for further development, amended applications and refinements upon previous practice, this area of home–school links needs to be carefully documented and continually revised. It is an area of practice that has political overtones and is linked to legislation. The researchers and practitioners are accountable at all local levels, to parents, governing bodies, the local authority, elected members and officers.

Why involve parents in schools?

The rationale for the myriad of projects has been reiterated in Chapters 2 and 4. The brief list below, taken from Rivalland (1989), is a reminder of these fundamental reasons, which can now be substantiated from direct experience. Fostering parental involvement in schools will provide benefits by:

- giving children a more effective learning environment, made possible through an increased adult:pupil ratio;
- providing schools with extra personnel and human resources;
- giving parents new insights and understanding about their children, as they build bridges between home learning and school learning;
- providing schools with parents who are knowledgeable about school needs.

Bastiani (1989) gives a list of reasons why parents volunteer to help in schools and classrooms, which includes:

- to help their own children;
- to help the school;
- to meet some of their own needs (p. 85).

At this point in the chapter a stocktaking exercise might be appropriate, to help to clarify thinking about the information provided so far and to identify in more depth some of the pros and cons of involving parents in schools. The perspective taken is that of the teacher, though readers could also, as a subsequent exercise, repeat it from the perspective of a parent.

EXERCISE: Preparing a balance sheet to help appraise the advantages and disadvantages of parental involvement in schools

Purpose: A vital precursor to such involvement is for teachers to examine their own attitudes towards, readiness for and commitment to working with parents. Your perceptions of the value of such joint work will be based on attitudes as well as on the evidence as to the effectiveness of such work.

What to do: Draw up two lists under these headings:
1   How can parents in schools positively help teachers to teach and children to learn?
2   How might parents in school threaten or compete with the teacher's role?

Comments: This exercise can be done on your own or in a group. Lists can be compared and discussed, and if the exercise is done in a group, one composite list can be compiled to represent a collective view. One outcome is to deepen understanding of the many and complex factors involved in parental involvement, and to balance *desirable* aspects against the *realities*. Hence the balance sheet idea.

AGE AND PHASE DIFFERENCES IN PARENTAL INVOLVEMENT IN SCHOOLS

Age and phase differences are significant. Before we can proceed with describing key areas we need to identify what they are and why they exist.

Generally it is reported that there is an increased amount of parental involvement in school, and reciprocally with home-based activities, in the earlier years; that is to say, in the pre-school and primary phases. It is commonly considered that teachers and parents have traditionally had closer contact in these years. At the nursery stage, parents usually bring children into school (or day nursery, or playgroup), so they are readily accessible. This obtains for some time at primary school, but an additional factor is that the organization of primary schools is more conducive to parent–teacher contact than is that at secondary level. It has proved more difficult to set up and maintain teacher–parent initiatives in secondary schools because:

- Such schools are bigger and more diffuse.
- More teachers are involved with more children, so the contact is fragmented.
- Homework has traditionally excluded parents in a formal sense (that is, parents may help, but their assistance has been informal and incidental).
- Parent–teacher contact has been formalized into set, arranged meetings, usually of the open-evening variety.
- Teachers who have trained to be subject specialists have not necessarily held an inclusive view of education; that is, one that embraces parents as educators. They see teaching (their subject) as their province.

Thus the bulk of the work has taken place in primary schools (Edwards and Redfern, 1988; Bryans, 1989; Stacey, 1991), though significant innovation has taken place in the early, pre-school years (Smith, 1980; Tizard *et al.*, 1980; Pugh, 1989; Hinton, 1989; Pugh and De'Ath, 1989).

At secondary level, there is a growing number of initiatives which have addressed some of the problems and limitations listed above. Examples include the following:

- Sandler (1989) describes PACE, a reading-focused scheme aimed at first-year secondary pupils, which branched out into other curriculum areas after establishing its credibility.
- Duncan (1989) relates how home, school and community come together within a racially diverse environment.
- Templeton (1989) traces the setting up, implementation and 'teething' of a home–school council in a south London comprehensive school, which was a key recommendation of the Hargreaves Report (1984) into secondary education in the Inner London Education Authority (ILEA).

In fact the now defunct (since 1 April 1990) ILEA spawned a number of home–school initiatives both at primary level (such as PACT: see Griffiths and Hamilton, 1984, 1987) and at secondary level. Arising from this experience, a book describing effective practice and providing guidelines was produced (Harding and Pike, 1988), targeted at secondary schools. It covers: first contacts; face-to-face contact; written communication; assessment; parent-governors; parent organizations; links with agencies; parental involvement in the life of the school, including learning.

The transition from primary to secondary is, as we know, a crucial time of change and adjustment for children. Parents can play a supportive role at this stage: Bastiani (1989) refers to 'key moments', defined as 'particular events and special occasions, often deliberately sought or organized' (p. 98). He goes on:

> It is at times like these, such as starting or changing schools, that relationships are made or broken, when important attitudes or patterns of behaviour are laid down for the future. So the idea of 'key moments' can be a useful one in the exploration of home–school thinking across a broad area. (p. 98)

What follows is a focus on a number of key areas which illustrate parents in schools. They range from curriculum and behaviour support (the mirror image of home-based learning and support programmes described in Chapter 4), to parental representation on governing bodies and associations, to other ways in which parents work with teachers in school. They are ways in which school is both a microcosm and a representative of the wider community.

PARENTAL INVOLVEMENT IN READING (PIR)

The school-based element is the counterpart to home-based literacy and reading activities, and stems essentially from the reading and literacy programmes in schools. For maximum effectiveness the one must complement the other. This is no mere rhetoric: one major reason why PIR initiatives started was that school and home did not necessarily pull together on this fundamental curriculum area. The main elements of contemporary schemes are outlined in Chapter 4 in some detail.

From a school perspective, a tremendous amount of planning, organization and monitoring is necessary to start and sustain a programme. It is not necessary to reiterate here the list of such endeavours, taken from Topping and Wolfendale (1985), which was presented in Chapter 4. More appropriate for a chapter representing the school perspective is to call attention to the need, endorsed by an increasing number of practitioners in this area, for schools to have not only a policy on the teaching of reading (as part of the teaching of English, a National Curriculum core area) but a whole-school policy on involving parents in reading and literacy (Topping, 1989). A number of recent reports on teaching reading have highlighted the part that parents can play. The HMI survey (1991b) states, 'The quality and extent of parents' support for children's reading had a positive effect on their standards of reading' (p. 12, para. 62), and reports that about two-fifths of the schools surveyed had successfully developed co-operative approaches with parents 'on an impressive level' (*ibid.*). This range of linked activities was described: curriculum meetings, home visits, booklets, videos, demonstrations of reading approaches, open days, book weeks, book fairs, school book shops and parent lending libraries with books about reading.

A reverse observation is made in the NFER survey into reading (DES, 1991), commissioned by the Department of Education and Science in the wake of the controversy about reading standards referred to in Chapter 4. A number of local education authorities reported to the NFER researchers that a 'lack of parental involvement' could be contributing to the alleged decline in standards, but, as the researchers themselves say, this aspect needs further exploration. A House of Commons Select Committee, also investigating the reading standards phenomenon during 1991, urged greater parent–teacher collaboration in this area.

So there appears to be a consensus that 'parents as educators' can make a significant contribution to children's acquisition of reading and literacy skills. Indeed, there is much that parents routinely do at home in terms of verbal interaction with their children (see Chapter 4) that is compatible with the profile components and attainment targets of English as a National Curriculum core subject – see particularly 'speaking and listening' as well as, obviously, 'reading'. While teachers would legitimately say that they have, on the whole, traditionally taught to these targets, it remains the case that the National Curriculum provides an articulated framework, and is therefore conducive to the maintenance of co-operative ventures between teachers, parents and children themselves.

PARENTS AND OTHER CURRICULUM AREAS

Maths and numeracy were examined in Chapter 4, in terms of what parents can do at home, routinely and/or via a special programme, to support their children's acquisition of number concepts. The programme that has to date had widest take-up has been IMPACT, which was discussed in Chapter 4 (see Merttens and Vass, 1990), though many primary schools have for years used a parent–teacher forum to explain new-maths approaches to parents. Many of us recall that our own attainment in mathematics lagged behind competence in literacy skills, as parents attested in Edwards and Redfern (1988). After one such parent–teacher session, where teachers explained maths teaching, some parents said that they understood for the first time what maths was all about and had enjoyed the moments when they had grasped the concepts.

Like English, mathematics as a National Curriculum core subject lends itself, in its structures and sequences, to linked school and home programmes. Approaches such as IMPACT can acquire increased validity when linked explicitly with teaching maths from Year One.

The areas of reading/literacy and mathematics/numeracy have provided not only the major exemplars of the effectiveness of linked school–home learning programmes, but also methodologies which have been replicated in other curriculum areas, as has been reported (see references already cited in this chapter). A key requisite for schools embarking on the involvement of parents in the curriculum (beyond the three National Curriculum core subject areas) in terms of planning, input and joint evaluation of outcomes is to be clear about the purpose and the nature of the joint enterprise. There are potentially a number of spin-offs, as we have seen, but, as Bastiani (1989) makes clear, a mutual agenda at the outset is vital. In his conception, the agenda is a multifaceted one, comprising a number of key components which he sets out in diagrammatic form (Bastiani, 1989, p. 82). These include (moving clockwise around his diagram): reviewing the progress of individual children; involving parents in their own children's learning; involving parents in the learning and development of children in general; communicating about the curriculum; developing interest in, understanding of and support for the work of the school and wider educational issues; using parental skills, interests and knowledge as a curriculum resource; encouraging parents' own educational development. The centre of the diagram contains the title of the model: 'Involving parents in the curriculum: an agenda'.

BEHAVIOUR AND DISCIPLINE IN SCHOOL: THE PARENTAL CONTRIBUTION

The interface between home and school in this area of potential joint concern was initially explored in Chapter 4, mainly from the perspective of the home as a locus for behaviour change. Among the key recommendations of the Elton Report (reference in Chapter 4) were exhortations to include parents in developing policy and effective 'discipline in schools' practices. The Report contains a whole chapter devoted to home–school relationships, and deals with stresses upon parents and the need to support them in their child-rearing tasks (see Chapter 3) as well as exploring the concept of 'responsible parenthood'. This is an important key concept, since it mirrors the responsibility of schools to educate children, and paves the way for a parent–teacher working relationship based on *reciprocity* (see Wolfendale, 1983, Chapter 1, for definitions; also Chapter 1 of this book).

Several writers (for example, Atkinson, 1989) have outlined models for a whole-school approach to discipline, but as I argue elsewhere (Wolfendale, 1990), such a policy could be rendered less effective without the inclusion of parents in the decision-making and implementation processes. After all, schools' governing bodies retain responsibility for discipline as well as curriculum, so it is logical to subsume parents into this notion of collective responsibility (Macbeth, 1989).

PARENTS AS GOVERNORS AND GOVERNORS AS PARENTS

The 1980s saw a profound shift in power-sharing in and about schools, most notably via the composition of the governing bodies of schools. Successive legislation (1980 and 1986 Education Acts, 1988 Education Reform Act) ensured parental representation on school governing bodies, as well as teacher, local business and community representation. The exercising of individual and collective interests is still evolving as governing bodies learn not only how to work together but how to exercise their powers, duties and responsibilities (considerably enhanced by the aforementioned legislation, particularly the 1988 Education Reform Act).

Governors' duties now encompass staffing, including appointments as well as dismissals, finance (via LMS mechanisms), proper and effective delivery of the National Curriculum, special needs (see Chapter 7) and sex education. Thus they are accountable to the parents of schoolchildren, the teaching body, the LEA and the wider community. Forums for debate, discussion, dialogue with and reporting to this wider constituency include the mandatory governors' annual report and the annual meeting. For comprehensive accounts of the duties and responsibilities of governors, see Fowler (1989) and ACE (1990).

The parents' perspective is of course wider than just the parental representation on the governing body, since many of the other governors will also be parents. Hence the heading to this section – it is relevant to acknowledge that a parental view on any issue arising on the agenda can come from any parent who happens to be on the governing body, whatever his/her capacity. However, the parents who are on the governing body in the capacity of parent-representatives have a distinctly different representation and brief, which may be difficult to administer. The HMI survey (1991a) reported the positive news that in the majority of the seventy schools surveyed, parent-governors undertook the same tasks and responsibilities as their colleagues. A minority felt that they were not held in the same regard and were not equally involved in the work of the governing body.

Since there is no prescription for parents-as-governors, it is not surprising that there is no uniform way in which they and probably others perceive their role. It can incorporate any or all of the following:

- representation – speaking on behalf of all the parents of the school;
- safeguarding all the parents' interests;
- reflecting back to parents what decisions are made (conduit function);
- being a repository of information, derived from in-service training as well as presence on the governing body, which can be passed on.

Can parental representation on schools' governing bodies empower parents? The organization and composition of governing bodies are intended to be a microcosmic representation of democracy at work. The reality is that any power-sharing arrangement has the endemic potential (usually realized!) for in-fighting, jockeying for position and promoting self-interest. There should be sufficient checks and balances in the system for the various factions to have a chance to be heard and their views heeded as part of the decision-making process. But, irrespective of how articulate and *au fait* with the system any parent-representative might be, the fact that until so recently parents have been excluded from education means that the force that they collectively represent is taking time to establish itself. Also, there is much evidence (see references at the end of this chapter) that parent-governors who had not identified with school before continue to feel marginalized, even excluded from the procedures and routines of meetings – formalized agendas, minute-taking, etc.

Legislation has ensured that the parental vote is powerful, and parental opinion can be mobilized to bring about significant changes, including changes to school status (to grant-maintained). But such democratic forces require the electorate to be well informed, able to weigh and balance all the evidence surrounding a given issue, (relatively) prejudice free, able to articulate its views, and then capable of self-representation. The onus is on adequate recruitment and a satisfactory level of quality training and support systems to (all) governors, to enable them to carry out their duties. As a corollary to these increased duties, now enshrined in legislation, the Department of Education and Science issued recruitment leaflets designed to attract potential governors, particularly parents, and made grants available to support local education authorities to offer governor training. These facilities have to combat the inherent drawbacks of becoming a governor:

- increased information load – some would say overload;
- practical difficulties in attending the necessary in-service training;
- additional duties comprising a burden.

My personal experience of involvement in one LEA's governor in-service training programme over a number of years is that these drawbacks constitute a dilemma for governors and the LEA. For the good will and interest are there; governors (and particularly parent-governors?) have a vested interest in educational matters and are keen to participate, but they feel overwhelmed.

Given that these powers and duties do exist and must be exercised, how best can parent-governors be supported to represent other parents and, in so doing, become empowered to take 'good' decisions on behalf of children? They have a right to receive:

- up-to-date information;
- training that equips them to handle the levers of power along with the other governors;
- resources to enable them to represent the views and concerns of other parents fully;
- assurances that their views and those of others are accorded equal status.

These references are commended for further reading on the political, social and educational issues surrounding the governing of schools: Sallis (1988), Golby (1989), Macbeth (1989), Wragg and Partington (1989) and Stacey (1991). A thinking exercise follows, aimed at encouraging readers to reflect further on effective ways in which parent-governors can exercise their responsibilities.

EXERCISE: How parental views can be expressed to and through parent-governors

Purpose: To encourage reflection as to how parent-governors can ensure that they canvass and represent parental views.

What to do:
1   List some practical ways in which parent-governors can contact and communicate with all parents.
2   Then list issues and concerns that parents might have that could fall within the remit of parent-governors to represent and try to act upon.

Comments: This exercise is best done as a group discussion, so that participants can pool their existing knowledge. Do not worry if you do not feel very informed in this area – the brainstorming nature of this exercise will stand you in good stead when you come to read and learn more about what governors do in general.

KEEPING SCHOOLS OPEN AND ACCESSIBLE: ALIGNING PARENTAL INVOLVEMENT AND COMMUNITY EDUCATION

The parental presence has permeated so many areas of school life that it is difficult to see how the clock could be put back. Since this phenomenon is not unique to the UK, we can perhaps feel confident that 'parent power' is here to stay. But, as with the expression of rights in any sphere, it is not easy to predict the directions of change.

Schools have certainly become more open and accessible through a number of mechanisms and processes, including representation; and the government has legislated to introduce school inspection procedures which will include representation from the local business community. As the structure and organization of local government changes, schools become accountable to the community in different ways. The Citizen's Charter (see Chapters 8 and 9) sets out to confer rights and responsibilities upon all participants.

Parents remain, potentially if not in actuality, schools' best allies, so it behoves schools to include parents automatically in the equation of decision-making, not only in those spheres where parents now have voting rights (as, for example, when considering whether or not the school should become grant-maintained), but at all levels. We have enough examples of effective practice, as reported in this book and many others, but, as Bridges (1987) points out, there are always parents who do not come to school, seem not to respond to invitations to participate and appear unreachable.

Is there a formula which not only entices stay-away parents into school in such a way that they feel comfortable and 'at home' in school, but which also keeps a school community intact? According to Watt (1989), community education has not sufficiently embraced parental involvement. She holds that there have been parallel innovations in both these spheres without synthesis or integration: 'it is a matter of particular regret that community education has not been able to develop within schools a climate of cooperation, expertise and experience in parent involvement capable of dealing with recent government legislation on school management' (p. 182). There are different ways of interpreting and operating 'community education', and this diffuseness in practice means that, as Watt avers, there is no co-ordinated theory or agreed set of principles. This can be seen as a weakness at a time (such as now) when the whole education and local government system is in flux. What matters as far as the 'messages' of this book are concerned is that no parent is disadvantaged, marginalized or excluded because parental involvement initiatives in a given school are started casually or incidentally, without recourse to an articulated policy. The best protection for parents and schools alike is an alignment between community concepts, in which schools are part of and defined by their communities, and partnership with parents, in which proven practice is used as a springboard for continued co-operation and identifying shared goals.

Such a fusion is exemplified in the Strathclyde partnership (Kay and Struthers, undated; Grant, 1989) between the LEA, schools and parents, or in the Coventry Community Education Project (Widlake, 1986), or the Liverpool Parent Support Programme (Davis, 1987). As with Ray Phillips's case study in Chapter 10, such enterprises are epitomized by a mix of 'top-down' support (funding, administration and endorsement from officers) and grass-roots or 'street-level' commitment from parent-participants, who perceive their needs and work towards their empowerment through co-operation. It is to be hoped that all such work over recent years can inspire future joint ventures at this time of flux and change.

Three key concepts are highlighted from the many initiatives examined in this chapter which epitomize the character and intention of many:

RESPONSIBLE PARENTHOOD the idea that teachers and parents have dual and reciprocal responsibilities towards children and each other

PARENTAL REPRESENTATION the idea that parent-governors are a vehicle for conveying and acting upon parents' views and concerns

SCHOOL AS A COMMUNITY the idea that schools are defined by and are part of their local communities.

CHAPTER SUMMARY

This chapter has ranged over some of the many parental involvement-in-school initiatives including parents and the curriculum, discipline in schools, parents and governors, and schools as communities. The evidence from many sources attests to the strong presence and influence of parents in schools whilst at the same time pointing the way for continuing research in this area.

FURTHER READING

Grant, D. (1989) *Learning Relations*. London: Routledge. This is a vivid and first-hand account of the setting up and continuation over a number of years of the Govan/Strathclyde project. The book demonstrates the improvements in children's active learning when parents participate.

Wragg, E.C. and Partington, J.A. (1989) *A Handbook for School Governors*. 2nd edition. London: Routledge. This book provides a comprehensive introduction and guide to governors' duties and responsibilities, as well as comprising a practical guide to being an effective governor.

Wolfendale, S. (ed.) (1989) *Parental Involvement: Developing Networks between School, Home and Community*. London: Cassell. The synthesis between school, home and community is described in several chapters, while others describe successful parental involvement in school ventures at pre-school, primary and secondary levels.

REFERENCES

Advisory Centre for Education (ACE) (1990) *Governors' Handbook*. 2nd edition. London: ACE.

Atkinson, J. (1989) Responding to Elton: a whole school approach. *Support for Learning*, Vol. 4, No. 4, pp. 242–8.

Bastiani, J. (ed.) (1987) *Parents and Teachers*. Vol. 1. *Perspectives on Home–School Relations*. Windsor: NFER-Nelson.

Bastiani, J. (ed.) (1988) *Parents and Teachers*. Vol. 2. *From Policy to Practice*. Windsor: NFER-Nelson.

Bastiani, J. (1989) *Working with Parents: A Whole-school Approach*. Windsor: NFER-Nelson.

Bridges, D. (1987) It's the ones who never turn up that you really want to see – the 'problem' of the non-attending parent. In J. Bastiani (ed.), *Parents and Teachers*. Vol. 1. *Perspectives on Home–School Relations*. Windsor: NFER-Nelson.

Bryans, T. (1989) Parental involvement in primary schools: contemporary issues. Chapter 3 in S. Wolfendale (ed.), *Parental Involvement: Developing Networks between School, Home and Community*. London: Cassell.

Cullingford, C. (ed.) (1985) *Parents, Teachers and Schools*. London: Robert Royce.

Davis, J. (1987) Liverpool's parent support programme: a case study. Chapter 13 in G. Allen, J. Bastiani, I. Martin and K. Richards (eds), *Community Education: An Agenda for Educational Reform*. Milton Keynes: Open University Press.

Department of Education and Science (1991) *An Enquiry into LEA Evidence on Standards of Reading of 7 year old Children: A Report by the National Foundation for Educational Research*. London: DES.

Duncan, C. (1989) Home, school and community in a multiracial context. Chapter 6 in S. Wolfendale (ed.), *Parental Involvement: Developing Networks between School, Home and Community*. London: Cassell.

Edwards, V. and Redfern, A. (1988) *At Home in School*. London: Routledge.

Fowler, W.S. (1989) *Teachers, Parents and Governors: Their Duties and Rights in School*. London: Kogan Page.

Galvin, P., Mercer, S. and Costa, P. (1991) *Building a Better-behaved School*. Harlow: Longman.

Golby, M. (1989) Parent governorship in the new order. Chapter 7 in F. Macleod (ed.), *Parents and Schools: The Contemporary Challenge*. Lewes: Falmer.

Grant, D. (1989) *Learning Relations*. London: Routledge.

Griffiths, A. and Hamilton, D. (1984) *Parent, Teacher, Child*. London: Methuen.

Griffiths, A. and Hamilton, D. (1987) *Learning at Home*. London: Methuen.

Harding, J. and Pike, G. (1988) *Parental Involvement in Secondary Schools*. London: ILEA.

Hargreaves, D. (1984) *Improving Secondary Schools*. London: ILEA.

Hinton, S. (1989) Dimensions of parental involvement; easing the transfer from pre-school to primary. Chapter 2 in S. Wolfendale (ed.), *Parental Involvement: Developing Networks between School, Home and Community*. London: Cassell.

HMI (1991a) *Parents and Schools; Aspects of Parental Involvement in Primary and Secondary Schools, 1989–1990*. London: DES.

HMI (1991b) *The Teaching and Learning of Reading in Primary Schools*. London: DES.

Jowett, S., Baginsky, M. and MacNeil, M.M. (1991) *Building Bridges: Parental Involvement in Schools*. Windsor: NFER-Nelson.

Kay, I. and Struthers, S. (undated) *Partnership in Education: A Public Report*. Glasgow: Glasgow Education Department.

Macbeth, A. (1989) *Involving Parents: Effective Parent-Teacher Relations*. Oxford: Heinemann Educational.

Macbeth, A. and Munn, P. (1990) *Parents and Education: Priorities for Research*. Edinburgh: Scottish Council for Research in Education.

Macleod, F. (ed.) (1989) *Parents and Schools: The Contemporary Challenge*. Lewes: Falmer.

Mayall, B. (1990) *Parents in Secondary Education*. London: Calouste Gulbenkian Foundation.

Merttens, R. and Vass, J. (1990) *Bringing School Home: Children and Parents Learning Together*. London: Hodder & Stoughton.

Plewis, I., Mooney, A. and Creeser, R. (1990) Time on educational activities at home and educational progress in infant school. *British Journal of Educational Psychology*, Vol. 60, pp. 330–7.

Pugh, G. (1989) Parents and professionals in pre-school services: is partnership possible? Chapter 1 in S. Wolfendale (ed.), *Parental Involvement: Developing Networks between School, Home and Community*. London: Cassell.

Pugh, G. and De'Ath, E. (1989) *Working towards Partnership in the Early Years*. London: National Children's Bureau.

Rivalland, J. (1989) *Parents Helping in the Classroom*. Rozelle, New South Wales: Primary English Teaching Association.

Sallis, J. (1988) *Schools, Parents and Governors: A New Approach to Accountability*. London: Routledge.

Sallis, J. (1989) Involving parents in the school. In *Parents and Schools*, CASE Supplement No 7. Cambridge: CASE.

Sandler, A. (1989) PACE: parental involvement in a learning through reading programme. Chapter 4 in S. Wolfendale (ed.), *Parental Involvement: Developing Networks between School, Home and Community*. London: Cassell.

Smith, T. (1980) *Parents and Preschool*. London: Grant McIntyre.

Stacey, M. (1991) *Parents and Teachers Together*. Milton Keynes: Open University Press.

Templeton, J. (1989) Creation of a home school council in a secondary school. Chapter 5 in S. Wolfendale (ed.), *Parental Involvement: Developing Networks between School, Home and Community*. London: Cassell.

Tizard, B., Mortimore, J. and Burchell, B. (1980) *Involving Parents in Nursery and Infant Schools*. London: Grant McIntyre.

Topping, K. (1989) A whole school policy on parental involvement in reading. *Reading* (UKRA), Vol. 23, No. 2, pp. 85–97.

Topping, K. and Wolfendale, S. (eds) (1985) *Parental Involvement in Children's Reading*. London: Croom Helm.

Watt, J. (1989) Community education and parent involvement: a partnership in need of a theory. Chapter 10 in F. Macleod (ed.), *Parents and Schools: The Contemporary Challenge*. Lewes: Falmer.

Widlake, P. (1986) *Reducing Educational Disadvantage*. Milton Keynes: Open University Press.

Wolfendale, S. (1983) *Parental Participation in Children's Development and Education*. London: Gordon & Breach.

Wolfendale, S. (ed.) (1989) *Parental Involvement: Developing Networks between School, Home and Community*. London: Cassell.

Wolfendale, S. (1990) Involving parents in behaviour management – a whole-school approach. Chapter 15 in M. Scherer, I. Gersch and L. Fry (eds), *Meeting Disruptive Behaviour: Assessment, Intervention and Partnership*. Basingstoke: Macmillan.

Wolfendale, S. (1992) *Primary Schools and Special Needs: Policy, Planning and Provision*. 2nd edition. London: Cassell.

Wragg, E. C. and Partington, J. A. (1989) *A Handbook for School Governors*. London: Routledge.

ADDRESSES

Advisory Centre for Education (ACE), Victoria Park Square, London E2 9PB.

Campaign for the Advancement of State Education (CASE), c/o The Grove, 110 High Street, Sawston, Cambridge CB2 4HJ.

Calouste Gulbenkian Foundation, 98 Portland Place, London WIN 4ET.

ILEA, 275 Kennington Lane, London SE11 5Q7.

Primary English Teaching Association, PO Box 167, Rozelle, New South Wales 2039, Australia.

CHAPTER 6

Communication between parents and teachers over children's progress

CHAPTER OVERVIEW

The latter part of this chapter is focused more on practice than are other chapters. The main parts examine developments and thinking in the areas of written and verbal communication, schools' reporting upon children's progress to parents, and the parental contribution to assessment. The justification for then concentrating on how readers can appraise their existing skills in communication with a view to developing their competence is that *communication skills* are the binding elements in home–school relationships. Without effective means of initiating and conducting a dialogue between teachers and parents, other 'good ideas' (such as joint curriculum projects) are less likely to be successful. This chapter is positioned mid-way in the book quite intentionally; enough discussion has taken place so far to provide a context, and what emanates from this chapter can inform reading and thinking about the later chapters, and, I hope, even influence practice.

KEEPING PARENTS INFORMED

We have already noted how; historically, parents have been kept at arm's length from schools and, until recently, marginalized from education. From the beginning of the 1980s onwards, increasing attention has been paid to parents' needs and rights to be kept informed about school business as well as their children's progress.

On information from schools and the local education authority

The 1980 Education Act bound LEAs as well as schools to provide written information to parents about local educational provision generally and details about schools' organization, staffing, curriculum arrangements and provision. Although it is now standard for schools and LEAs to issue brochures, their quality (of appearance and content) varies widely, reflecting degrees of commitment. Sullivan (1988) has some practical suggestions to make about producing a quality product, and so has Bastiani (1989), whose comments are based on several years of researching this area and, with colleagues, experimenting with various blueprints.

At national level, the Department of Education and Science (DES), following government's own advice to LEAs and schools to provide parents with written information, published a booklet for parents entitled *Our Changing Schools* (1988a). This combined a number of strategies designed to help parents choose a school, get their children ready for school and help their children, with details about the 'new developments'; that is, the educational changes brought about by the 1988 Education Reform Act. This handbook was followed the following year by a leaflet for parents, *National Curriculum: A Guide for Parents*, and since then the DES has issued other guidance for parents (see below on reporting progress to parents). These moves at national as well as local level have been welcomed by parents, certainly, though it cannot be assumed that increased awareness by parents is necessarily widespread, as was confirmed by the DES parents' awareness survey and also by the Exeter survey, both reported in Chapter 2. The latter is referred to again later in this chapter.

Newsletters

Newsletters are an increasingly common means by which schools keep parents informed of school developments, plans and activities, and also sometimes solicit their involvement and support. Letters to parents are more 'user-friendly'; that is, the language is less formal and the tone more friendly, and in many multi-ethnic areas, letters, newsletters and even school magazines may be printed in local home-languages as well as English. Again, Sullivan (1988) and Bastiani (1989) provide illustrations from a variety of sources, as do Harding and Pike (1988) on the basis of work in the Inner London Education Authority.

Written reports to parents

The work of Goacher and Reid (1985) confirmed that there has long existed a consensus on the desirability of sending periodic reports home to parents about their children's progress, but there has been considerable debate about the best form for doing this. Earlier debate has been somewhat superseded by the requirements for schools reporting to parents contained in the 1988 Education Reform Act and subsequent guidance from the DES, which merits an entire section later in this chapter. Here we note not only the earlier work by Goacher and Reid and concerns raised several years ago about the then adequacy of school reports (DES, 1977), but also the comparative study undertaken by Macbeth (1989) into practice in the EC, which uncovered six types of written report: periodic; year-end; day books; communication booklets; curriculum progress and 'carnets de liaison'; and multi-purpose booklets.

Parental access to records

The opening-up process has extended progressively over the years to parental rights to access to school records on their children, subject to one or two safeguards; for example, in the case of children suspected of being abused (DES, 1988b). Recognition of parents' right to information was built into the 1981 Education Act (Special Educational Needs), which guarantees parents the receipt of the draft and final Statement of Needs as well as the professional reports (medical, educational, psychological) on which the Statement is based (see Chapter 7).

The various forms of written communication dealt with above do not replace but are complementary to direct, face-to-face contact such as meetings in school and home visiting.

Meetings in school

Teachers' timetables and parents' domestic and work commitments preclude spontaneous and incidental meetings, but the necessary formality of pre-arranged meetings is not always conducive to a satisfactory dialogue, as many parents and children can attest, having come away from a parents' evening. The basic purpose is of course information exchange, and Sullivan (1988) and Harding and Pike (1988), while acknowledging the obvious limitations, have practical suggestions to make to improve the occasion.

A simple exercise is suggested at this point to address this issue:

EXERCISE: thinking of ways of improving the parents' evening

Purpose: To consider how parents can be invited; what the agenda of the meeting could consist of; and how teachers can:

1   elicit information from parents;
2   impart information to parents;
3   record information.

What to do: Brainstorm 1, 2 and 3 and produce lists.

Comments: The points on the lists might be commonsense suggestions, but such matters are all part of good preparation for such an event.

Home visiting

Home–school liaison in the form of teachers visiting parents at home has been a feature of many of the parental involvement projects, particularly those with a community education focus (Chapters 2, 3, 4 and 5). Both provision of and opinion on home visiting as a viable means of promoting home–school links and encouraging parents as educators have been mixed and variable. Wolfendale (1983) raised the issue of whether, in a given school where one teacher has the brief and a special post for home liaison, this absolves the other teachers from responsibilities to promote home–school links. Macbeth (1989) explores this and other issues, while Sullivan (1988), Harding and Pike (1988) and Stacey (1991) explore the issues and offer practical suggestions and some solutions.

The reality is that, since the start of the major growth in home liaison and educational home visitor posts in the 1970s, there have been cutbacks; such posts are vulnerable at times of economic retrenchment. Yet, while they are not standard in schools, growth has continued in two particular areas of education. One is the appointment in a number of LEAs of 'outreach' teachers – those with a special brief to effect home liaison with ethnic minority families; the other is pre-school education and education for special educational needs (see Chapter 7).

Parent–teacher associations (PTAs)

Surveys over the last twenty years or so have confirmed that the majority of schools have PTAs or PTA equivalents; that is, a forum for teachers and parents to meet and engage in social and perhaps fund-raising activities. Each school defines and uses its PTA in its own way. For example, in a secondary school in south London parents did not feel that the PTA was an adequate forum for encouraging a full and honest dialogue, and so took on board one of the recommendations in the Hargreaves Report for a home–school council (Templeton, 1989).

The current reality is that fund-raising constitutes a major activity of a PTA, though the parent organization, the National Confederation of Parent Teacher Associations (NCPTA; address at end of Chapter 2) produces literature on a wide range of topics and attempts to influence educational thinking and practice at a national level. Macbeth (1989), alert to the limitations as well as the potential of this kind of teacher–parent forum, has proposed several alternative approaches, each of which he believes has advantages and disadvantages: a parents' association, an education association, and a mini-association (discussed in Chapter 7 of his book). He relates these possibilities to the context of the 1988 Education Reform Act, outlining how a PTA-equivalent could provide mechanisms for dealing with such issues as open enrolment, opting out and Local Management of Schools.

In this section, we have looked at the various ways in which teachers and parents communicate in written and verbal form. The subject matter of their dialogue ranges legitimately across many areas, from the need to improve the school's resources (fund-raising focus), to school plans and activities, to curriculum development and dialogue about children's progress. This last area has always been a linchpin of discussion between teachers and parents, but recent developments are significant enough for it to merit a section on its own. This itself is split into two parts, the first examining how teachers report upon pupils' progress to parents and the second exploring the parental contribution to assessment and reporting. Essentially the emphasis of the whole section is on demonstrating how interactive and reciprocal the nature of such information exchange is, or should be.

ASSESSING AND REPORTING UPON PUPILS' PROGRESS

Reporting to parents

It was mentioned above that there are various traditional as well as new ways in which teachers communicate with parents about how their children are faring in school. The Goacher and Reid study (1985) slightly predated but paved the way for significant changes in the written report, particularly as these researchers had identified a number of limitations to the traditional approaches.

Focus on assessment

The methods of reporting debate have been brought to prominence by developments in assessment thinking and practice. Two of the most important developments have been Records of Achievement (see below) and arrangements for a national system of assessment as a corollary of the National Curriculum, both being central planks of the 1988 Education Reform Act (ERA).

The ERA sets much store by parents' right to access to information about their children's progress. Various means are encouraged; for example, the use of Records of Achievement and home–school diaries. Traditional written report formats could continue to be used, but realistically are superseded by the new requirements (see below).

The developments and issues in assessment (educational, social and political) are examined by Gipps (1990). What is to the point for the purposes of this book is to acknowledge a consensus that parents have a need and a right to assessment information, whatever the form and purposes of assessment. The Task Group on Assessment and Testing (TGAT, 1988) said, 'Assessment is at the heart of the process of promoting children's learning', a view not only endorsed by the government but integral to the ERA. As the DES in *National Curriculum: From Policy to Practice* (1989) reiterated, assessment serves these four purposes: formative, summative, informative, and helpful for professional development. The same document goes on to outline what the various *purposes* of assessment are, including:

- to give parents the information necessary to support an informed dialogue with the school . . .
- to enable a school to report on the overall achievements of its pupils in ways that not only parents but also the wider community can appreciate. (Sections 6 and 7)

What information do parents want?

Goacher and Reid's study (1985) confirmed that parents positively wanted and welcomed a written report, but that 'what parents very often lacked, however, was any guidance as to exactly how they could help their child to do better' (p. 158). According to Harding and Pike (1988), parents may have views about: the form of reports which they would find helpful; frequency of reports; which aspects of their child's progress should be reported upon; the criteria used for assessment; and what contributions they as parents could make.

These views accord with the research carried out by Patricia Broadfoot (1989), who reports on some New Zealand research which explored parents' views as to the information they would like to receive from teachers. They said that they wanted comments which were:

- achievement oriented;
- factual;
- positive;
- broadly based;
- free of speculation and able to be substantiated;
- significant;
- related to learning goals;
- succinct;
- constructive.

During a one-day conference entitled 'Assessment – The Parental Dimension', held in one London borough during 1991, at which the participants were mostly primary school headteachers, the question was put to them, 'What do parents want from reporting and assessment?' Many of the participants had the dual perspective of being teacher and parent, and this list typifies the responses:

1   to know what the school will do next as a result of assessment and what parents can do in co-operation;
2   arising from 1: to be able to discuss the previous year's report with the subsequent year's teacher;
3   positive comments on progress both in relation to previous performance and that of other children – parents will often register negative comments too easily;
4   positive strategies which the school intends to implement to correct or improve deficits;
5   to know that their child is happy in school.

(This is verbatim: acknowledgements and thanks to the London Borough of Sutton Education Department.)

The broader context to the receipt by parents of written information from school has to be their knowledge, awareness and understanding of the purposes of assessment. As part of their study 'Parents and the National Curriculum', referred to in Chapter 2, Hughes *et al.* (1991, 1992) report on parents' knowledge of and reactions to the Standard Assessment Tasks (SATs). Findings at this stage of the implementation of SATs as well as the National Curriculum are bound to be equivocal; that is, as Hughes and his colleagues report, there is wide variation in understanding and awareness. These early findings do, however, serve as a reminder that schools have to make every effort to provide parents with the necessary background information to the specific information about their child's progress.

The new requirements

Under the ERA, schools have mandatory duties to report to parents and to provide them with an annual written report on their child's achievements, covering National Curriculum (NC) subjects, public examination results (if appropriate) and other school subjects and activities. During 1991 the DES issued to all schools a letter (20 March) accompanied by a model format for such reports. This was intended as a model, not a prescription. It contains sections for all NC and other curriculum areas, plus space for 'overview of performance' and 'recommendations for action by parents'. The guideline is explicit that the report should pave the way for fuller discussion with the parent, not be a substitute for it. In April 1992 the DES issued a circular (DES, 1992).

Also, during 1991 the DES provided a leaflet for teachers, *Reporting to Parents: Some Suggestions for Primary Teachers*, which urged them to follow up the report with further discussion and meetings with parents. Again during 1991, three leaflets for parents were issued by the DES: *Your Child's Report – What It Means and How It Can Help; How Is Your Child Doing at School – A Parents' Guide to Testing;* and *Your Child and the National Curriculum.* The recent spate of official information directed at parents is unprecedented and represents an acknowledgement that unless parents are sufficiently informed they will remain marginalized; and worse, from a school's point of view, that teachers will not get the backing they need from parents for their teaching endeavours.

A comprehensive system of reporting to parents

We have seen how parents are quite clear about what information they want about their children's progress. The new requirements would not in themselves go far enough in fulfilling parents' needs for a range of information if the model format were adopted, mainly because there is space only for summative assessment, not for formative and contextual information. So the DES itself encourages the adoption in schools of Records of Achievement systems.

The history of the piloting and evaluation of Records of Achievement (RoA), mainly but not exclusively in secondary schools, has been well documented (Broadfoot, 1988). RoAs are now established as being a flexible tool for the recording of all sorts of curriculum information as well as of other activities, in and out of school, with which a pupil may be engaged – all from a number of perspectives; that is, teachers', pupils' and parents'. The parental dimension has had least attention paid to it to date, but there are signs that the potential for inclusion of the parental perspective is being realized in some schemes (and see the next section).

Certainly RoAs are intended to be shown, sent or given to parents. For example, the National Record of Achievement, issued jointly by the Department of Employment and the Department of Education and Science for the first time during 1991 for that year's school-leavers, contains a leaflet for parents.

The DES Circular 8/90 (DES, 1990) on Records of Achievement was quite clear that one prime purpose of schools' using them is to pass information on to parents. Consistently with this message, the School Examinations and Assessment Council (SEAC) published at the end of 1990 a guidance booklet largely comprising a number of examples of good practice in primary schools. Already a number of local education authorities have initiated an LEA-wide RoA system, and they include parents. For example, Sheffield LEA has trialled and adopted a RoA system for primary education, involving parents in the recording process (Thompson and Desforges, 1991; Desforges, 1991). The verbal and written dialogue between teachers and parents on the assessment and monitoring of children's progress in and out of school is a paramount feature.

We turn now to the parental element of this equation – what parents can contribute directly to assessment and reporting.

The parental dimension to assessment: towards 'reciprocal reporting'

A significant growth area in the last few years has been that of parental input to assessment, mainly within the special educational needs sphere (and see Chapter 7), but increasingly within early child development and education, especially primary.

It is quite consistent with the many innovative parent–professional programmes described in earlier chapters that new ways of involving parents in the appraisal and monitoring of their children's development, progress and learning should be trialled and some approaches adopted into pre- and primary-school practice. Some of these will be described. First, however, it is relevant to recapitulate on some fundamental purposes of assessment which embrace the parental perspective, and then to consider what skills parents bring to acts of assessment which could be said to complement professional skills.

Assessment as a partnership between, say, teachers and parents can be conceived of in broad terms:

- It encompasses the earliest stages of parents and professionals exchanging and sharing information and beginning to list their views and concerns about a child.
- It includes a later stage at which data are collected, recorded and exchanged in systematic ways by teachers (and other professionals working with children) and parents.
- It can incorporate informal approaches such as observation, discussion and the use of checklists as well as formal means such as standardized tests (less desirable and nowadays less relied upon).
- It can constitute a continuing process throughout parent–teacher relations, in the sense that the partners in the enterprise will maintain contact, share concerns, report upon progress as well as problems, jointly celebrate success, and monitor and review events.

The data from joint initiatives suggest that the quality of content of parental input is equal to that of trained professionals and that the information is complementary, as it is derived from different sources (home, school) representing the different settings in which children spend their lives, and describes their behaviour in these different learning and social milieux. Evidence confirms that 'untutored' parents can abstract salient facts and features about their child in the home context and report upon these orally and in writing.

For a review of the research evidence and the principles behind this growing area of practice, see Wolfendale (1988). Evidence of the effectiveness of this partnership comes from a range of sources: the PIP developmental charts (Jeffree and McConkey, 1976), the Portage check list (see Wolfendale, 1990, for discussion), and the Oxfordshire Health Authority-pioneered personal child health record (Talbot, 1988; Elfer and Gatiss, 1990). To summarize what such research and practice have found, both in educational (see below) and non-educational settings:

- Parents have expertise in commenting on development.
- Parents' intimate knowledge of their children can be described by them.
- Parental information can complement professional information.
- The information can show up differing behaviour in different settings.
- The information can serve to highlight concerns regarding progress.
- Parents can provide a realistic appraisal of their children.

Elsewhere (Wolfendale, 1988) I have summarized the particular skills that parents bring to assessment, on the basis of my collaborative action-research into parental profiling – the writing of 'profiles' of their children by parents as a contribution to Section 5 Assessment under the 1981 Education Act (special needs). The many acts and actions parents undertake routinely when rearing and interacting with their children, which are part and parcel of daily and continuing 'assessment' of children by their parents, include observing, predicting, describing and reporting. Data from the profiling study reported in Wolfendale (1988) led to the revision of the guidelines for parents, which are now routinely available in many LEAs (contact the author for further information at the Psychology Department, University of East London). These, as well as subsequent workshops, have elicited considerable information about the skills and experience that parents bring to assessment. Overall they can be subsumed under these headings: knowledge of developmental areas; family, contextual and background knowledge; parenting functions (Wolfendale, 1991a, contains further discussion on these experiences and skills).

Implications for school-based assessment and a partnership with parents

We have seen the premium that has been placed by the government and the Department of Education and Science (via ERA requirements and circulars) on keeping parents informed of their children's progress in school. Many of the developments cited above, including Records of Achievement, include mechanisms for informing parents about the curriculum and assessment (SATs and school-based assessment), but, laudable as these are, they tend to fall short of direct inclusion of the parental view and perspective. Few to date elicit more than parents' comments on information provided by the school, as against the additional dimension of information on how the child is faring at home – a vital corollary to the school data.

There are several examples of recent and current work that demonstrate the potential, realized in practice, of assessment approaches which incorporate the dual perspective on equal terms. Hugh Waller, in one of the case studies in Chapter 11, describes work in hand in a primary school in Bournemouth. The present author (Wolfendale, 1991b) describes work in a number of LEAs as well as pre-school settings on the adoption of ALL ABOUT ME, a developmental profile completed by parents in partnership with teachers (and other professionals such as childminders; see Davies, 1991). This profile was first piloted extensively, then evaluated and revised (Wolfendale, 1987), and subsequently piloted as a 'point of entry' to school profile (Bone, 1990). At the time of writing, it is being similarly piloted in the London Borough of Newham (see Wolfendale, 1991b, for a summary of the work to date). See also the use of development diaries (Ollis, 1990), the Buckinghamshire Observation Procedure (1990) and the inservice materials developed in Warwickshire (Warwickshire County Council, 1992; see also Chapter 10).

The precedent is available, then, for all schools to move to their own versions of the model of reciprocal reporting first outlined in Wolfendale (1991a), the basic philosophy of which is: utilization of equivalent expertise; mutual and complementary exchange of information and concerns; and the use of assessment approaches by parents and teachers as a vehicle for promoting educational opportunity for each and every child.

DEVELOPING COMPETENCE IN COMMUNICATING WITH PARENTS

It was asserted at the very beginning of this chapter that communication skills are the binding elements in home–school relationships. In order for teacher-practitioners to conduct their dialogue with parents effectively via the gamut of mechanisms described in this chapter, a certain amount of competence in several fundamental areas is crucial. Little sustained training is included in initial or even inservice training on these issues, as has been noted in Chapter 2. Yet the people-focused skills of initiating and sustaining dialogue, listening, responding sensitively, working co-operatively to an agenda and shared problem-solving could be said to be as important as training to teach a subject.

The assumption is made in this section that each reader will already possess a range of relevant skills in these areas, but all of us need, from time to time, to reappraise our competence and assess the extent to which we might benefit from changing our style and consciously developing competence in some ways. So this chapter, which has ranged widely over many areas of direct interface between teachers and parents, concludes with seven practical exercises, which encourage such reappraisal and also provide strategies for skill improvement in face-to-face contact with parents. The exercises are:

> What are teachers like with parents?
> Setting the scene – relaxing with each other
> Encouraging parents to talk
> Developing listening skills
> Showing and sharing feelings
> Preparing to discuss matters of concern
> Closing the conversation and appreciating each other.

They range from initiating, to sustaining, to closing contact and dialogue.

EXERCISE: What are teachers like with parents?

Purpose: To appraise your attitudes to parents

What to do: Consider the statements below. You can comment Yes/No/Sometimes on each:

* I am a good listener.
* I consider parents' point of view.
* I look at them directly when we speak.
* I ask questions and show I am interested.
* I make time to see parents.
* I do not interrupt.
* I do not blame them for any difficulties.
* I tell them as much as possible about their child.
* I give advice sensitively.
* Parents can rely on me.

Comments: This exercise can be done singly, then discussed with others. The activity can provide a useful starting point for discovering your own attitudes.

EXERCISE: Setting the scene – relaxing with each other

Purpose: This is more of a reflective exercise, encouraging you to think about and plan a setting conducive to a good meeting.

What to do: Consider:

* the seating arrangements;

* how people will sit;
* their physical comfort;
* whether refreshment is available.

Comments: This activity may encourage reflection on how to create an atmosphere in which you and parents can feel relaxed, and parents can feel welcome.

EXERCISE: Encouraging parents to talk

Purpose: Brainstorm some ways in which you can encourage others to talk, discuss and disclose. Here are some suggestions:

* Agree an agenda at the outset.
* Ask general social questions to put the other person at ease.
* Make encouraging comments.
* Reflect back to the other person (feedback and comment).
* Probe sensitively to draw the other person out.
* Ask 'open' questions to encourage the person to provide information beyond 'Yes' or 'No'.

Comments: These are some of the social strategies you can employ. You could practise them in couples or small groups.

EXERCISE: Developing listening skills

Purpose: This exercise is designed to help you decide how good a listener you are and to improve your skills.

What to do: 1. Brainstorm some bad listening habits. How about:

* sitting tensely;
* looking impatient;
* looking away;
* looking at your watch;
* interrupting;
* fiddling with paper-clips, papers or jewellery.

2. Read the statements below and comment on each *Yes/No/ Sometimes*:

* I look directly at the other person.
* I concentrate on what the other person is saying.
* I show interest in what the other person is saying.
* I ask questions, listen to the answers and reflect back.
* I am patient and polite.
* I have a friendly, warm, sympathetic attitude.
* I know when to stop talking.
* I take turns; that is, ask questions, listen and talk in turn.

Comments: We are not all automatically good listeners and we could all benefit from activities which encourage us to decide how good we are at listening and how we could improve.

EXERCISE: Showing and sharing feelings

Purpose: This exercise is designed to help you to express and control a range of feelings, including strongly felt and negative ones.

What to do: Share your feelings about school in a small group. Tell each other what good/bad memories you have of your own school-days and of your favourite/most disliked teachers.

Comments: This discussion activity is only an example of how you can identify, examine, discuss and perhaps control strong emotion.

EXERCISE: Preparing to discuss matters of concern

Purpose: There will be occasions when teachers and parents need to meet to discuss issues over a child that worries, concerns or angers one or both parties.

What to do:

*   Agree an agenda.
*   Remember and apply 'normal', polite social behaviour even when you/the other person are expressing emotions.
*   Signal early on to the parent, 'There is something I would like to discuss' – do not delay this moment.

Can you think of other 'tips' to help handle the situation?

Comments: Anticipating a difficult situation undoubtedly helps to deal with it.

EXERCISE: Closing the conversation and appreciating each other

Purpose: To end a dialogue on a positive note.

What to do: Consider these reasons for needing to end a meeting on a positive note:

*   needing to agree what has been discussed;
*   needing to agree future action;
*   needing to thank each other for sparing time to talk and share;
*   needing to confirm to each other that you have valued this opportunity to meet.

Comments: This activity sounds like common sense, and so it is, but it provides a stocktake of sensible action with which to close a meeting on a constructive note and to maintain a positive dialogue.

This chapter has introduced several key concepts:

> **PARENTAL PROFILING** the contribution that parents can make to assessment
>
> **RECIPROCAL REPORTING** the idea that information exchange is of mutual benefit to teachers and parents, based on 'equivalent expertise' and in the interests of children
>
> **COMMUNICATION COMPETENCE** effective communication skills are the building blocks to productive dialogue with parents.

CHAPTER SUMMARY

The chapter has comprised a mix of discussion and review with presentation of a number of practical strategies in the form of exercises, designed to improve communication skills to enhance the teacher–parent dialogue. Various ways in which teachers could communicate with parents in verbal and written form have been described, within the context of the 'new requirements', including methods of reporting to each other how children are progressing.

FURTHER READING

Atkin, J., Bastiani, J. and Goode, J. (1988) *Listening to Parents: An Approach to the Improvement of Home–School Relations*. London: Croom Helm. The emphasis in this book is on fostering effective parent–teacher relationships via a whole range of strategies which include, as a key element, listening to and heeding the parental voice.

McConkey, R. (1985) *Working with Parents: A Practical Guide for Teachers and Therapists*. London: Croom Helm. As its title implies, this is a practice-focused book on how to set up one-to-one meetings as well as parent groups and courses, and how to give talks, use video, etc.

SEAC (School Examinations and Assessment Council (1990) *Records of Achievement in Primary Schools*. London: HMSO. This is a booklet of guidance to support developments in recording and reporting achievement. By the use of many examples, it aims to reflect current practice by teachers, in some instances involving parents.

Wolfendale, S. (1988) *The Parental Contribution to Assessment*. Developing Horizons No. 10. Stratford-upon-Avon: National Council for Special Education (now the National Association for Special Educational Needs). This pamphlet provides a review of research and applications into the parental contribution to assessment, including a detailed description of the first national pilot study into the use of guidelines to assist parents to write a parental profile of their child.

REFERENCES

Atkin, J., Bastiani, J. and Goode, J. (1988) *Listening to Parents: An Approach to the Improvement of Home–School Relations*. London: Croom Helm.

Bastiani, J. (1989) *Working with Parents: A Whole-school Approach*. Windsor: NFER-Nelson.

Bone, S. (1990) 'The report of the London Borough of Bexley pilot of the ALL ABOUT ME as a point of entry profile'. Unpublished MSc Educational Psychology dissertation, Psychology Department, University of East London.

Broadfoot, P. (1988) *Records of Achievement: Report of the National Evaluation of Pilot Schemes*. London: HMSO.

Broadfoot, P. (1989) *Reporting to Parents on Student Achievement: The UK Experience*. Working Paper No. 2/89, October. Bristol University.

Buckinghamshire Observation Procedure (1990) Aylesbury: Buckinghamshire Education Department.

Davies, A. (1991) 'An evaluation of the use of ALL ABOUT ME with childminders and parents'. Unpublished MSc Educational Psychology dissertation, Psychology Department, University of East London.

Department of Education and Science (DES) (1977) *Education in Schools*. London: HMSO.

Department of Education and Science (DES) (1988a) *Our Changing Schools*. London: HMSO.

Department of Education and Science (DES) (1988b) *Working Together for the Protection of Children from Abuse: Procedures within the Education Service*. Circular 4/88, July. London: DES.

Department of Education and Science (DES) (1989) *National Curriculum: From Policy to Practice*. London: HMSO.

Department of Education and Science (DES) (1990) *Records of Achievement*. Circular 8/90, July. London: DES.

Department of Education and Science (DES) (1992) *Reporting Pupils' Achievements to Parents*. Circular 5/92, April. London: DES.

Desforges, M. (1991) National Curriculum assessment and primary records of achievement, tensions and resolution. Chapter 1 in G. A.

Lindsay and A. Miller (eds), *Psychological Services for Primary Schools*. Harlow: Longman.

Elfer, P. and Gatiss, S. (1990) *Charting Child Health Services*. London: National Children's Bureau.

Gipps, C. (1990) *Assessment: A Teachers' Guide to the Issues*. London: Hodder & Stoughton.

Goacher, B. and Reid, M. (1985) *School Reports to Parents*. Windsor: NFER-Nelson.

Harding, J. and Pike, G. (1988) *Parental Involvement in Secondary Schools: A Guide for Reviewing Practice and Developing Policy*. London: ILEA.

Hughes, M., Wikeley, F. and Nash, T. (1991, 1992) *Parents and SATs*. Interim Reports from the project 'Parents and the National Curriculum'. Exeter: School of Education, University of Exeter.

Jeffree, D. and McConkey, R. (1976) *PIP Developmental Charts*. London: Hodder & Stoughton.

Macbeth, A. (1989) *Involving Parents: Effective Parent–teacher Relations*. Oxford: Heinemann Educational.

McConkey, R. (1985) *Working with Parents: A Practical Guide for Teachers and Therapists*. London: Croom Helm.

Ollis, J. (1990) Parent-held development diaries in practice. *Early Years*, Vol. 10, No. 2, pp. 20–7.

SEAC (School Examinations and Assessment Council) (1990) *Records of Achievement in Primary Schools*. London: HMSO.

Stacey, M. (1991) *Parents and Teachers Together*. Milton Keynes: Open University Press.

Sullivan, M. (1988) *Parents and Schools*. Leamington Spa: Scholastic Publications.

Talbot, M. (1988) Parent-held child health records. *Primary Health Care*, November, pp. 14–15.

Templeton, J. (1989) Creation of a home school council in a secondary school. Chapter 5 in S. Wolfendale (ed.), *Parental Involvement: Developing Networks between School, Home and Community*. London: Cassell.

Thompson, D. and Desforges, M. (1991) Assessment in the National Curriculum and primary records of achievement: some impossibilities and tensions. *British Psychological Society Division of Educational and Child Psychology Newsletter*, No 44, pp. 29–36.

Warwickshire County Council (1992) 'Reporting to Parents': INSET materials. Leamington Spa: EDS Publications.

Wolfendale, S. (1983) *Parental Participation in Children's Development and Progress*. London: Gordon & Breach.

Wolfendale, S. (1987) The evaluation and revision of the ALL ABOUT ME pre-school parent-completed scales. *Early Child Development and Care*, Vol. 29, pp. 473–558.

Wolfendale, S. (1988) *The Parental Contribution to Assessment*.

Developing Horizons No. 10. Stratford-upon-Avon: National Council for Special Education (now the National Association for Special Educational Needs).

Wolfendale, S. (1990) ALL ABOUT ME. Nottingham: Nottingham Educational Supplies.

Wolfendale, S. (1991a) Parents and teachers working together on the assessment of children's progress. In G. A. Lindsay and A. Miller (eds), *Psychological Services for Primary Schools*. Harlow: Longman.

Wolfendale, S. (1991b) Involving parents in assessment and appraisal: a description of the development and applications of ALL ABOUT ME. *Positive Teaching*, Vol. 2, No. 1, pp. 23–30.

ADDRESSES

Buckinghamshire Education Department, County Hall, Aylesbury, Bucks. HP10 1UZ.

EDS Publications, Manor Hall, Sandy Lane, Leamington Spa, War. CV32 6RD.

Nottingham Educational Supplies, Ludlow Hill Road, West Bridgford, Nottingham NG2 6HD.

CHAPTER 7

Parents, equal opportunities and inclusive education

CHAPTER OVERVIEW

This chapter is in three parts. The first deals with overarching concepts and themes to do with equal opportunities, rights and needs of children and the place of parents in delivering equality policies. The rest of the chapter examines two of the major equal opportunities issues. So the second section briefly traces the evolution of race equality in education, with a view to appraising the extent to which parents have been involved in initiatives; and the third section looks at special educational needs and disability issues, again appraising the extent to which parents have been involved in recent and continuing developments. Overall common elements between these important areas are identified with regard to parental rights and participation.

CONCEPTS AND THEMES

The reader might be wondering why two allegedly important areas, equal opportunities for children from ethnic minorities and equal opportunities for children with special educational needs, are not being accorded a chapter each in this book. The reason is that, as Mittler explains (1989), 'the special needs and multicultural lobbies have much in common' (p. 196). He elaborates this point by saying, 'Both are aiming to achieve a higher quality education not only for the children in their "constituency" but for all children. Both are concerned with the effects of teacher under-expectation and under-demand' (p. 196).

Although each of the two lobbies identified by Mittler can and does 'fight its own corner' to achieve parity of esteem, full equality of opportunity, and elimination of discriminating, even prejudiced practice, it can serve a different but, one hopes, equal purpose to unite the two areas. Historically, over a number of years, both were marginalized from the mainstream of education, and even now they need their vigilant advocates to ensure that the needs are met and the rights recognized of children from ethnic minorities and children with special educational needs.

The reader may also appreciate that these two areas remain contentious, and the trap of writing about them is to be drawn into categorizing the children who appear to 'belong' in one or both of the two areas. It would indeed be invidious so to do, but at the same time the case is made for calling attention to the fundamental principle of *entitlement* now enshrined in the Education Reform Act (ERA), which is intended to apply *to all children*. The justification as far as this book is concerned is as follows:

- There have to be agreed pedagogical and pastoral mechanisms to ensure that pupils who may be vulnerable in school for any reason have access to, and can therefore take up their full rights to, curriculum entitlement.
- We have sufficient accumulated evidence, as we have seen from the subject matter of the previous six chapters, that parental participation in education is advantageous to children.

So we need to ensure that parents of children from ethnic minorities and those with special educational needs feel welcome in and are welcomed into school, and can and do make a significant contribution, from their own distinctive perspectives, to their children's education as well as to school life generally.

Becoming aware of equal opportunities

During the last twenty years or so we have witnessed and participated in changes of attitude and practice towards those children who, at worst, used to be discriminated against and, at best, were included in school life without their particular situation being addressed. As far as children from different ethnic, cultural and religious backgrounds are concerned, educational responses have, in recent years, included provision for English as a second language, consideration of bi- and multilingualism, and strategies to eliminate racism. For children with special needs or disability, there is not only the protection of legislation in the 1981 Education Act, but also the increasing sophistication of curriculum and intervention techniques, as well as a growing commitment (in some quarters, not all) to integrated educational provision. These changes are picked up once more in the next two parts.

A number of key concepts underpin the philosophy and practices:

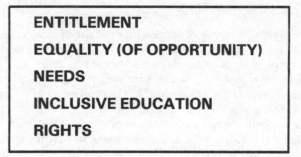

ENTITLEMENT

EQUALITY (OF OPPORTUNITY)

NEEDS

INCLUSIVE EDUCATION

RIGHTS

Although these key concepts have been presented in a list, they could equally be shown as a web, demonstrating their interlocking nature. Each of these fundamental concepts in education has been or is being operationalized to a greater or lesser extent. The best way of explaining this point further is to cast some light upon the definition of each of these and provide examples.

Entitlement

'Entitlement' usually refers, certainly at present, to the principle that all children have an entitlement, an inalienable right, to access to and receipt of the school curriculum and, as is spelled out by the DES (1989), especially to the National Curriculum. The concept of entitlement in educational contexts is, in the eyes of the government which initiated the Education Reform Act, related to schools' responsibilities to provide and deliver a broad and balanced curriculum which will 'promote the spiritual, moral, cultural, mental and physical development of pupils at the school and of society' and 'prepare such pupils for the opportunities, responsibilities and experiences of adult life' (DES, 1989, p. 2).

Although, as a 'given' set of precepts, it is unlikely that people would take much issue with these responsibilities, Kelly (1990) urges us to be wary of operating them at face value. He reminds us that 'any curriculum will reflect the values of its creators', and goes on, 'and the imposition of those values on all pupils, whatever their background and origins, even in the name of equality, must be . . . a highly questionable form of practice' (p. 119). The dilemma, as Kelly perceives it, rests on the entitlement of all children to a common (national) curriculum, which, however, to meet individual needs, will have to be differentiated, if not tailor-made for each child.

However, the strength and power of this concept may well lie in the fact that, although previous Education Acts have contained the principle of entitlement for *all* children, the Education Reform Act properly spells it out, and so, in the eyes of children, their parents and teachers, is the bedrock principle.

Equality (of opportunity)

The principle of equality of opportunity is defined as meaning that no child should be excluded from or denied access to the fullest possible available range of educational opportunities. It is an advance on previous educational thinking, which held that the curriculum and extra-curricular activities were on offer, but that no especial effort need be made to ensure that all children could in fact take them up. The match between curriculum and child was not made – the history of remedial education exemplifies this. For many years and until recently, children with reading or learning difficulties were 'withdrawn' from their classes at designated times (once or twice a week, say) to receive remedial teaching and support in small groups. Little attempt was made by teachers to ensure liaison between class and remedial teaching. Thus the 'remedial' child was, paradoxically, denied access to the full range of educational opportunities, under the guise of being treated differently. This did not advantage him/her, as was the intention, but marginalized the 'failing' child even more (Wolfendale, 1992). Now the principle acknowledges that every effort must be made to ensure that children classically denied access to all facets of school life – whether by disability (physical, or severe or moderate learning difficulties, for example), race (without commensurate language provision and a truly multicultural education, children from ethnic minorities, particularly those who were not born in the UK, have been disadvantaged), gender or poverty (two equal opportunities issues not dealt with here) – are fully embraced into the mainstream by whatever means it takes.

Roaf and Bines (1989) recognize how inequality has operated over many years, structurally, institutionally and interpersonally in the major areas of race, class, sex and disability. It takes time and complex provision to dismantle inequitability, and, as Roaf and Bines say, 'equal opportunity is also an effective touchstone for evaluating provision' (p. 11). Their specific context is that of special educational needs and disability, but the principle is generalizable, and Boyd (1989) reiterates it: 'Equality is essentially a practical principle that has everything to do with rights being established over the fair distribution of valued resources' (p. 42). He goes on to acknowledge the same dilemma that Kelly identified (see above).

Needs

That the concept of 'needs' has been, over a number of years, a problematic one has been acknowledged by several writers, from Wolfendale and Bryans (1979) to Roaf and Bines (1989). The classic exposition of the universality of all children's needs is by Kellmer-Pringle (1975), whose *The Needs of Children* outlined a fourfold classification: the need for love and security; the need for new experiences; the need for praise and recognition; and the need for responsibility. The usual demarcation is between universal physical needs for shelter, warmth and food, all necessary for survival, and universal psychological needs, conceptualized much as Kellmer-Pringle did, which ought to be met in order to guarantee emotional adjustment, well-being and growth.

The problematic aspect of the concept of needs is to do with the fact that these constructs and necessaries are value-laden and culture-bound. Although there is broad agreement about what children need to survive and grow, there is less consensus about the means to meet these identified needs. So one view in the disability area, espousing integrated education as a means of meeting individual needs, is countered by an opposing view holding that the needs of children with developmental, learning and physical difficulties are 'special' and different, and can best be met in separate and protective settings. Likewise, to exemplify the point from the race equality area, the debate continues to rage as to whether or not children from ethnic minorities, British-born or not, have different, distinctive and 'special' needs simply 'because' they come from classifiably 'ethnic minority' families (see Wolfendale, 1983, Appendix for a discussion of these issues).

A recent critical analysis of the concept of 'need' is given by Woodhead (1991), who demonstrates how the concept has been differently defined in a number of key documents and reports that span twenty years and include the 1989 Children Act, the most recent legislation to contain its own definition of 'need'. These sources emanate from different disciplines; thus it is not surprising that there is no one agreed definition. Woodhead challenges what he perceives to be an unspoken assumption that all children's needs are universal, whereas, in fact, 'while in certain very general respects "need" statements may have universal validity, detailed prescriptions about children's needs are normative and depend on a judgement about processes of cultural adaptation and social adjustment' (Woodhead, 1991, p. 48). One of his main 'messages' is to urge people working with children, especially (in the context of his chapter) with young children, to take such cultural imperatives on board, and not to use the term 'need', which does have validity, glibly as a blanket term.

The implication of this brief analysis of this key concept, within the context of this book, is that parents must be centrally involved with teachers and other professionals in assessing and identifying children's needs within and in relation to the context of the children's circumstances and experiences to date.

Inclusive education

In one way, the term 'inclusive education' represents a restatement and reworking of the original concept of *comprehensive* education, but its current usage refers to the broadest possible connotation of *integrated* education, especial emphasis being given to the inclusion of children with special educational needs and disabilities in mainstream schools. Integration is ostensibly enshrined in the law of the land by the 1981 Education Act, but progress towards what is still an ideal rather than a universal reality remains halting and patchy, and the provisions contained in the 1988 Education Reform Act, such as Local Management of Schools, do little to hasten the advent of integrated education nation-wide. The variable commitment at local level, combined with instances of successful integration of children with special needs into mainstream education, has been well chronicled (Barton and Tomlinson, 1981, 1984; Booth and Swann, 1987; Lewis, 1991).

The specific concept of *inclusive* education emphasizes full participation in school and community life, but embraces, too, the means of achieving this goal. The London Borough of Newham, one of the very first LEAs to make a public commitment to integrated education during the 1980s, made an explicit commitment to inclusive education in 1991. The LEA sees this as a logical extension to the earlier stance on integration, since inclusive education represents the realization of equal opportunities, to which, in its broadest sense, the local authority has had a long-standing commitment. As inclusive education calls for fundamental attitude reappraisal and a collective will to dismantle structures that wittingly or unwittingly deny access to all opportunities for some children, it seems appropriate to perceive it as applying not only in the special-needs spheres from whence the concept emanated, but for children from richly diverse cultural and religious backgrounds.

So defining the relevance of curricular and non-curricular in-school experiences for children seems to be the collective responsibility of parents and families as well as of educationalists, through processes of empowering parents to be centrally involved in defining what education should offer their children.

Rights

The final key concept in this section, that of 'rights', appropriately follows from the others, for the expression in practice of entitlement, equal opportunities, inclusive education and the meeting of needs presupposes that the basic *rights* exist to bring these about. Also, a concept of human rights is the underpinning philosophy that has driven a number of prime movers within education and community circles (Cameron and Sturge-Moore, 1990; Rieser and Mason, 1990).

There is increasing agreement that statements on the rights of children provide guarantees and safeguards, though for these to have any force or effect there needs to be legislation or at least some equivalent powerful mandate. The United Nations Convention on the Rights of the Child is looked to by many people, representing a whole range of interest groups around the world, to have that kind of force and influence. It was passed in 1989, entered into international law in September 1990 and by early 1992 had been signed by a majority of countries, including (towards the end of 1991) the UK (Newell, 1991). The Convention covers four broad areas of rights – survival rights, development rights, protection rights and participation rights – and contains fifty-four articles, many of which concern education. Indeed, a number of writers (Trump, 1991; Wolfendale *et al.*, 1992) express the hope that rights commitments could be built into equal-opportunities policies to guarantee that the voice and view of the child are heard and heeded, and as a means of redistributing power.

Implications for parents of the key concepts

As we have seen from the review in preceding chapters of the variety of ways in which parents are involved in school and with their children's education, these initiatives tend to be discrete, concentrating on specific or particular curriculum areas. There have been fewer examples of 'wholist' parental involvement simultaneously on a number of fronts – though a few initiatives along these lines have been trail-blazers: see the case studies in Chapters 10 and 11. The kind of whole-school parental involvement advocated by Bastiani (1989; and see Chapters 8 and 9) may be propelled by the consumerist approach inherent in the Education Reform Act.

But whatever the impetus for continuing to involve parents in a range of activities, it is their own right to be party to contemporary thinking about equal opportunities, to understand the concept of curriculum entitlement, and to have integrated and inclusive education fully explained to them. For years, their participation in education has been on the terms of educationalists, who have retained superior powers and been privy to classified information. If those of us in education are going to take our responsibilities for creating quality education seriously, we can proceed no further, in this newer climate of accountability and quality assurance procedures, without the equal participation of informed parents who understand the philosophy as well as the practice.

In order to give readers an opportunity to pause and reflect upon these abstract concepts, an exercise is now offered which is intended to encourage thinking about implementing children's rights in education.

EXERCISE: Considering pupils' rights in school

Purpose: To appraise the extent to which pupils currently have rights when in school which are acknowledged and acted upon, and if they do not have such rights, to consider what rights they might be given and how they could be implemented.

What to do: This exercise is best done in pairs or small groups.

1 Choose a phase of education (primary or secondary, depending upon your training, experience and preference).
2 List the main areas of school life, such as classroom, curriculum, playground, etc.
3 Then, for each of these main areas, think of and list what pupils' rights could be.

Comments: The important thing in this exercise is to think about *rights* of pupils, rather than, at this point, to come up with a perfect solution or formula as to how teachers could ensure the rights could be realized in practice. That would be an ambitious undertaking, and the purpose of this exercise is simply to stimulate thinking in this area.

RACE EQUALITY, MULTICULTURAL EDUCATION AND PARENTS' PLACE AND CONTRIBUTION

The basic premise of this section is that in all the recent developments and initiatives in the UK concerning anti-racism and multicultural education, parents have been less consulted and involved, with few exceptions, than they might or should have been, but that it is still timely for them to become more centrally involved in these equal opportunities issues.

Extensive literature exists chronicling the developments and the thinking behind them in the areas of multicultural education (Arora and Duncan, 1986; Grugeon and Woods, 1990), theories of multi-ethnic education (Banks, 1988), the issues and politics of multiracial education (Sarup, 1986), prejudice and racism (Aboud, 1988; Kelly and Cohn, 1988; Troyna and Carrington, 1990), race, schooling and the ERA (Hardy and Vieler-Porter, 1990) and educational attainments (Verma and Pumphrey, 1988). But the parental dimension has not loomed large in these texts, in terms of the vital part parents could play in promoting truly multi-ethnic education or eliminating racist behaviour. Indeed, the Swann Report (1985), ostensibly a seminal report, omits mention of this important area.

However, despite the fact that parents, particularly those coming from an ethnic minority, have not yet achieved a central position in equal opportunities policy implementation, there has been sufficient attention given to this issue by a small number of writers and educationalists to provide strategies and models for this to be adopted on a wider scale than hitherto. Both I (Wolfendale, 1983, Appendix) and Tomlinson (1984) are at pains to emphasize that separate home–school policies for ethnic minority families would be separatist, invidious and ultimately racist. The proposition that both Tomlinson and I originally put forward was that the distinctive needs of pupils from ethnic minority backgrounds could be seen to be temporal and transitional; that is, families settling into another country and lifestyle were entitled to particular and sensitive consideration and treatment at a time in their lives marked by adjustment, transition and necessary acculturalization. Reciprocally, it behoved educationalists at the time of most significant immigration to accommodate to such societal phenomena and shift attitudes and practices accordingly, to prevent personal as well as institutional racism.

That racism in schools has not been eradicated and true race equality has not occurred to a significant extent can possibly be attributed to the absence of parents in decision-making and commensurate strategies. However, this is a speculative and retrospective hypothesis, and the purpose of this section, in the context of this chapter, is to be positive and forward-looking. So we can work within the frameworks of different models of parental partnership in general to ensure the maximum participation of all parents. On the basis of equal opportunities, we can apply differential strategies sensitively to draw in parents who were educated in other countries, whose first language may not be English and who, above all, need to feel welcome in and be welcomed into the formal institution of school.

However, we need to step cautiously into this arena. It would be simplistic to suggest blanket 'affirmative action' and promote the interests of 'minority' parents without acknowledging the constraints upon them: for example, even when welcomed into school, they have been expected to operate within structures that at worst are alien and at best just unfamiliar. Granados Johnson *et al.* (1989) point out that the traditional parent–teacher association 'termly meeting may intimidate many parents who find its middle-class structure of officers and agendas and articulate speakers alien' (p. 116); and, as pointed out in Chapter 5, this applies to parents as governors too. Likewise, Tomlinson (1987) cautions that 'minority home–school contact is the point at which basic values can clash and seemingly irreconcilable interests present themselves' (p. 215).

A mismatch between home and school expectations based upon prior lack of familiarity can of course extend to the curriculum, as Tizard *et al.* (1988) point out. Their particular example, based on their research, was that the Asian and West Indian parents in their sample just did not understand, and had not had explained to them, the 'learning through play' approach of British nursery and infant classes.

Finally, in highlighting some of the evident barriers to equitable parental participation, wherein ethnic minority parents have been most disadvantaged, let us see how Vassen (1986) summarizes the situation. He bases his view on his appraisal of anti-racist, multicultural policies in several London primary schools:

> Lack of involvement has three main strands. First, the unwillingness of teachers to participate with parents who are regarded as 'non professionals' and thereby not qualified to offer anything. Second, the notion that parents' duties cease at the school gate. Third, the schools' rigidity in structuring visits that do not take into account the work commitments of parents. (p. 131)

Fortunately, there are examples of good practice and plenty of ideas of utilizing the knowledge and skills of (all) parents to promote a pluralist perspective within schools, and to enhance and enrich children's knowledge about each other.

The broadest context in which to promote this partnership is of course that of community, and Duncan (1989) provides a working model of the close, symbiotic relationship between a local, multi-ethnic community and the secondary school that serves that community. He lists a whole range of options which epitomize such a fusion. Links with the local community are also advocated by Carrington and Short (1989) and Harding and Pike (1988), who also urge schools to include parents in setting, monitoring and reviewing in-school anti-racist strategies. Other writers, such as Granados Johnson *et al.* (1989), suggest school-based parents' support and interest groups. See also the HMI survey (1989) for examples of effective practice from three case study LEAs.

In these ways and over time, collective confidence among parents grows, and accumulating experience and familiarity with school can be shared with each other. Reciprocally, teachers can make a commensurate shift and can benefit from insights into a range of cultural, linguistic and religious backgrounds. Thus all the participants in the enterprise are enabled and empowered to operate equal opportunities and, in partnership, remain vigilant to ensure that these are adhered to.

The following exercise provides an opportunity to address the question of how some of the ideas could be put into practice.

EXERCISE: How teachers and parents can work together to eradicate racism in schools

Purpose: To think of strategies to effect reduction and elimination of racist attitudes and behaviour.

What to do:

1   Brainstorm and list the ways racism manifests itself in school (give examples of verbal and physical behaviour).
2   Consider how you would approach parents to become involved in anti-racism work.
3   List some ideas for joint work in this area.

Comments: This exercise provides a challenge to think of sensitive ways in which parents and teachers can deal with one another over a contentious issue.

SPECIAL NEEDS, DISABILITY AND PARENTS' PLACE AND CONTRIBUTION

The area of special needs and disability presents us with a situation in which there are many examples of innovative work involving parents in assessment and intervention, and we now have workable models and methodologies from a number of partnership ventures between parents and professionals. Also, as we shall see, there has been a significant rise in the number and type of self-help parents' groups. However, to the regret of those parents and professionals committed to partnership, such practice is not yet widespread, and the inclusion of parents of children with special needs in decision-making is not yet routine.

The purpose of this section is to sketch the main developments briefly (the area being well documented), and to emphasize the potential of consulting and involving parents at all levels of debate and decision-making to do with concerns over children's development and learning, their adjustment, their needs, placement, and adequacy of educational provision and resources. Like the other major issue studied in this chapter, this area is presented as an equal opportunities issue: that is, parents of children designated as having special needs are entitled to be treated equally; to have access to information about the school's curriculum (national and overall) and pastoral provision; to share in early exchange of concerns; to be consulted about appropriate help and support on offer within school and from support services; to be equal parties to decisions about referral for formal assessment under the 1981 Education Act; and to be involved in the ensuing action. As was stated earlier in the chapter, this is a human rights issue (Cameron and Sturge-Moore, 1990; Rieser and Mason, 1990).

That special needs and disability have gained a higher profile in education is generally acknowledged, and a number of writers have traced the growth of the provision, role and function of special needs advisory and support teachers, the increasing sophistication of techniques and equipment, the range of in-service courses, and the increasing adoption of special needs whole-school policies (Hegarty, 1987; Sayer, 1987; Wolfendale, 1987; Solity and Raybould, 1988; Thomas and Feiler, 1988; Mongon *et al.*, 1989; Montgomery, 1990; Norwich, 1990). Governors' duties in respect of special educational needs have increased, which helps to keep the issues on the educational agenda (Wolfendale *et al.*, 1990).

Attitudes towards the 1981 Education Act as an encourager of increased parental participation in special needs and disability issues have been divided. There are those who aver that the parents' rights contained in the legislation are actually quite limited, and those who regard the Act as a facilitator of parental involvement. The 'truth' is of course a mix of these stances, as the evidence from surveys and reports (Select Committee, 1987) confirms. As with any shifts in attitudes and provision, emerging good practice coexists, sometimes in dynamic tension, with traditional attitudes and practices.

A number of writers, researchers and practitioners have described their own and others' work in the areas of most significant practice change (Newson and Hipgrave, 1982; Mittler and McConachie, 1983; Wolfendale, 1983; Cunningham and Davis, 1985; Vaughan, 1989; Russell, 1990). Several of these publications describe work in discrete areas, where the shared expertise of parents and professionals has led to fruitful partnerships (McConachie, 1986; Wells, 1989). For a study which explores parent–professional communication in the context of the 1981 Education Act, see Sandow *et al.* (1987).

By way of exemplifying proven and emerging practice, several of the main areas of parent–professional co-operation will be briefly highlighted below.

Involving parents in the assessment process

The previous chapter discusses more fully in general educational terms how parents can be involved in the assessment process. The advent of the 1981 Education Act provided the spur to considerable work in the special educational needs and disability areas; for example, the work on parental profiling (see Wolfendale, 1988, which describes my work as well as that of others; see also Cunningham and Davis, 1985). Whatever the actual medium chosen – writing a parental profile, compiling a child report, completing a checklist, keeping a diary – the parental perspective on a child's development and learning and the expression of parental concerns and views can be included. Appendices in Wolfendale (1988) contain many extracts from completed parental profiles.

A major DES-funded project under way at the Voluntary Council for Handicapped Children is 'Partnership in Assessment', which is: drawing together good practice; establishing dialogue between parents and professionals on assessment, via in-service training courses (Stobbs, 1990) which emphasize multidisciplinary involvement and partnership between statutory and voluntary agencies; and developing a code of practice (contact Philippa Russell or Philippa Stobbs at VCHC, National Children's Bureau, 8 Wakley Street, London EC1 7QE).

Parents as key agents in intervention with children

The broad area of parents as key agents in intervention with children encompasses not only curriculum intervention but also many aspects of service delivery in which the parental contribution is acknowledged, valued and integral. Elfer and Gatiss (1990) describe many such initiatives: Portage, health and developmental surveillance, and the organization and running of toy libraries, playgroups and parent and community groups.

The best-developed and most written-about project is that of Portage, which exemplifies many aspects of good practice in partnership between parents and professionals from education, health, social services and voluntary agencies. It is a home-based learning programme for young children with learning difficulties and developmental delay, which involves parents as educators. Parental skills in use and in evidence on a daily basis include assessment, teaching, recording, monitoring, planning and evaluating. As Hanvey and Russell (1990) write:

> Portage is becoming a major source of skill training (and skill sharing) for professionals as well as for parents. Health visitors, community nurses, care workers, home liaison teachers and psychologists have learned through Portage how to work as a team, how to share ideas and skills directly with parents, and the importance of mutual support in selecting appropriate goals and teaching techniques for children with a wide range of special needs. (p. 23)

However, they and others point out that such effective practice does not and should not come 'on the cheap', and appropriate financing of such proven ventures of course continues to be an issue.

Parents' groups

Parents' groups are a significant development that has been charted by Wolfendale (1989, Chapter 8), who describes initiatives such as:

- the formation of local support and training ventures, sometimes involving voluntary and professional workers too, such as SNAP and PIP (see addresses at end of chapter; see also the case study by Ray Phillips in Chapter 10).
- the advent of the national umbrella organization 81 NETWORK (see addresses at end of chapter);
- the parent-to-parent scheme (Hornby, 1988).

See also the resource pack *Families and Self-help* (De'Ath and Webster, 1989). Collective action along these lines is a demonstrable force for empowerment by parents.

Empowerment can also, of course, come about through knowledge and familiarity with the procedures and the provision. Parents have written for other parents in an attempt to share experience as well as to encourage them to take action on behalf of their children (Kimpton, 1990; Goodey, 1991). Professionals, too, have written for parents (as well as co-professionals) in the same spirit (McConkey, 1985; Furneaux, 1988).

In the present climate, largely because of the advent of Local Management of Schools, not only is provision for special educational needs uncertain (Evans and Lunt, 1990) but the whole future of integrated education is in question. The government has signalled its intention to amend the 1981 Act during 1992–93 and to streamline assessment and appeals procedures. Yet there is much that vigilant parents and professionals committed to parental involvement can do to ensure full entitlement of children to all curriculum opportunities (Lewis, 1991; Russell, 1991) and to insist upon expression of their rights.

A discussion exercise, designed to explore some of these ramifications, now follows.

EXERCISE: To explore the potential of partnership with parents over special educational needs

Purpose: To encourage reflection as to effective ways of establishing a dialogue and developing strategies.

What to do: In pairs or a small group, think of ways in which teachers can ensure that parents are fully consulted and involved in discussion and decisions over children whose progress is causing concern and/or who have special educational needs or a disability.

Comments: This is an open-ended, exploratory exercise designed to stimulate thinking and appraisal of your attitudes to the rights of children with special needs, and to the rights of their parents to be centrally involved in discussion and planning.

CHAPTER SUMMARY

The key theme of this chapter has been the enumeration of the rights and entitlement of parents and children, particularly in areas where they have hitherto been neglected or marginalized. The two major areas described in the chapter have been race/ethnicity and special needs/disability. An *inclusive* philosophy has been promoted, in which parents are central to educational decision-making on behalf of their own children and as representatives of the whole parent body.

FURTHER READING

The general list of references for this chapter is long, as two areas, each important in its own right, have been brought together so as to make, I hope, a powerful case for parental rights. Three texts are singled out for further reading, not because they emphasize parental involvement necessarily, but because each of them epitomizes the two 'case study' areas dealt with in the chapter, and will stimulate reflection on issues of equality and rights.

Boyd, J. (1989). *Equality Issues in Primary Schools*. London: Paul Chapman.
Cole, M. (ed.) (1989) *Education for Equality*. London: Routledge.
Roaf, C. and Bines, H. (eds) (1989) *Needs, Rights and Opportunities*. Lewes: Falmer.

REFERENCES

Aboud, F. (1988) *Children and Prejudice*. Oxford: Basil Blackwell.
Arora, R. and Duncan, C. (eds) (1986) *Multicultural Education: Towards Good Practice*. London: Routledge.
Banks, J. (1988) *Multiethnic Education: Theory and Practice*. 2nd edition. London: Allyn & Bacon.
Barton, L. and Tomlinson, S. (eds) (1981) *Special Education: Policy, Practices and Social Issues*. London: Harper & Row.
Barton, L. and Tomlinson, S. (eds) (1984) *Special Education and Social Interests*. London: Croom Helm.
Bastiani, J. (ed.) (1988) *Parents and Teachers*. Vol. 2. *From Policy to Practice*. Windsor: NFER-Nelson.
Bastiani, J. (1989) *Working with Parents: A Whole-school Approach*. Windsor: NFER-Nelson.
Booth, T. and Swann, W. (eds) (1987) *Including Pupils with Disabilities*. Milton Keynes: Open University Press.
Boyd, J. (1989) *Equality Issues in Primary Schools*. London: Paul Chapman.
Cameron, J. and Sturge-Moore, L. (1990) *Ordinary Everyday Families: A Human Rights Issue: Action for Families and their Young Children with Special Needs, Disabilities and Learning Difficulties*. London: MENCAP.
Carrington, B. and Short, G. (1989) *'Race' and the Primary School: Theory into Practice*. Windsor: NFER-Nelson.
Cunningham, C. and Davis, H. (1985) *Working with Parents: Frame-*

works for Collaboration. Milton Keynes: Open University Press.

De'Ath, E. and Webster, G. (1989) *Families and Self-help: A Resource Pack*. London: National Children's Bureau.

Department of Education and Science (1989) *National Curriculum: From Policy to Practice*. London: DES.

Duncan, C. (1989) Home, school and community in a multiracial context. Chapter 6 in S. Wolfendale (ed.), *Parental Involvement: Developing Networks between School, Home and Community*. London: Cassell.

Elfer, P. and Gatiss, S. (1990) *Charting Child Health Services*. London: National Children's Bureau.

Evans, J. and Lunt, I. (1990) *Local Management of Schools and Special Educational Needs*. Report of a Conference. London: Institute of Education, London University.

Furneaux, B. (1988) *Special Parents*. Milton Keynes: Open University Press.

Goodey, C. (ed.) (1991) *Living in the Real World: Families Speak about Down's Syndrome*. London: Newham Parents' Centre.

Granados Johnson, J., Helliwell, J., Nicholson, J., Reay, D., Schwarz, H. and Wright, G. (1989) The infant years. Chapter 6 in M. Cole (ed.), *Education for Equality: Some Guidelines for Good Practice*. London: Routledge.

Grugeon, E. and Woods, P. (1990) *Educating All: Multicultural Perspectives in the Primary School*. London: Routledge.

Hanvey, C. and Russell, P. (1990) *Workbook 4: Children with Special Needs*, K254: Working with Children and Young People. Milton Keynes: The Open University.

Harding, J. and Pike, G. (1988) *Parental Involvement in Secondary Schools*. London: ILEA.

Hardy, J. and Vieler-Porter, C. (1990) Race, schooling and the 1988 Education Reform Act. Chapter 10 in M. Flude and M. Hammer (eds), *The Education Reform Act 1988: Its Origins and Implications*. Lewes: Falmer.

Hegarty, S. (1987) *Meeting Special Educational Needs in the Ordinary School*. London: Cassell.

HMI (1989) *A Survey of Parent–School Liaison in Primary and Secondary Schools Serving Ethnically Diverse Areas within 3 LEAs*. A report by HMI. London: DES.

Hornby, G. (1988) Launching parent-to-parent schemes. *British Journal of Special Education*, Vol. 15, No. 2, pp. 77–9.

Kellmer-Pringle, M. (1975) *The Needs of Children*. London: Hutchinson.

Kelly, A.V. (1990) *The National Curriculum: A Critical Review*. London: Paul Chapman.

Kelly, E. and Cohn, T. (1988) *Racism in Schools: New Research Evidence*. Stoke-on-Trent: Trentham Books.

Kimpton, D. (1990) *A Special Child in the Family: Living with your Sick or Disabled Child*. London: Sheldon Press.

Lewis, A. (1991) *Primary Special Needs and the National Curriculum*. London: Routledge.

McConachie, H. (1986) *Parents and Mentally Handicapped Children: A Review of Research Issues*. London: Croom Helm.

McConkey, R. (1985) *Working with Parents: A Practical Guide for Teachers and Therapists*. London: Croom Helm.

Mittler, P. (1989) Warnock and Swann: similarities and differences. Chapter 11 in G. Verma (ed.), *Education for All: A Landmark in Pluralism*. Lewes: Falmer.

Mittler, P. and McConachie, H. (eds) (1983) *Parents, Professionals and Mentally Handicapped People*. London: Croom Helm.

Mongon, D., Hart, S., Ace, C. and Rawlings, A. (1989) *Improving Classroom Behaviour: New Directions for Teachers and Pupils*. London: Cassell.

Montgomery, D. (1990) *Children with Learning Difficulties*. London: Cassell.

Newell, P. (1991) *The UN Convention and Children's Rights in the UK*. London: National Children's Bureau.

Newson, E. and Hipgrave, T. (1982) *Getting Through to your Handicapped Child*. Cambridge: Cambridge University Press.

Norwich, B. (1990) *Reappraising Special Needs Education*. London: Cassell.

Rieser, R. and Mason, M. (1990) *Disability Equality in the Classroom: A Human Rights Issue*. Inner London Education Authority.

Roaf, C. and Bines, H. (eds) (1989) *Needs, Rights and Opportunities*. Lewes: Falmer.

Russell, P. (1990) Policy and practice for young children with special educational needs: changes and challenges. *Support for Learning*, Vol. 5, No. 2, pp. 98–106.

Russell, P. (1991) Access to the National Curriculum for parents. Chapter 11 in R. Ashdown, B. Carpenter and K. Bovair (eds), *The Curriculum Challenge: Access to the National Curriculum for Pupils with Learning Difficulties*. Lewes: Falmer.

Sandow, S., Stafford, D. and Stafford, P. (1987) *An Agreed Understanding? Parent–Professional Communication and the 1981 Education Act*. Windsor: NFER-Nelson.

Sarup, M. (1986) *The Politics of Multiracial Education*. London: Routledge.

Sayer, J. (1987) *Secondary Schools for All? Strategies for Special Needs*. London: Cassell.

Select Committee (1987) *Special Educational Needs: Implementation of the Education Act 1981*. Vol. 1. Third Report from the Education, Science and Arts Committee 1986–87. London: HMSO.

Solity, J. and Raybould, E. (1988) *A Teacher's Guide To Special Needs:*

A Positive Response to the 1981 Education Act. Milton Keynes: Open University Press.

Stobbs, P. (1990) *Partnership in Assessment.* Paper given at the International Special Education Congress, Cardiff 1990. London: National Children's Bureau.

Swann, Lord (1985) *Education for All.* Report of the Committee of Inquiry into the Education of Children from Ethnic Minority Groups. London: HMSO.

Thomas, G. and Feiler, A. (eds) (1988) *Planning for Special Needs: A Whole-school Approach.* Oxford: Basil Blackwell.

Tizard, B., Mortimore, J. and Burchell, B. (1988) Involving parents from minority groups. In J. Bastiani (ed.), *Parents and Teachers 2: From Policy to Practice.* Windsor: NFER-Nelson.

Tomlinson, S. (1984) *Home and School in Multicultural Britain.* London: Batsford.

Tomlinson, S. (1987) Home, school and community. In J. Bastiani (ed.), *Parents and Teachers.* Vol. 1. *Perspectives on Home–School Relations.* Windsor: NFER-Nelson.

Troyna, B. and Carrington, B. (1990) *Education, Racism and Reform.* London: Routledge.

Trump, L. (1991) The UN Convention on Children's Rights – progress or fallacy? *Educational Psychology in Practice,* Vol. 7, No. 2, pp. 106–11.

Vassen, T. (1986) Curriculum considerations in the primary school. In J. Gundara, C. Jones and K. Kimberley (eds), *Racism, Diversity and Education.* London: Hodder & Stoughton.

Vaughan, M. (1989) Parents, children and the legal framework. Chapter 3 in C. Roaf and H. Bines (eds), *Needs, Rights and Opportunities.* Lewes: Falmer.

Verma, G. and Pumphrey, P. (eds) (1988) *Educational Attainments: Issues and Outcomes in Multicultural Education.* Lewes: Falmer.

Wells, I. (1989) Parents and education for severe learning difficulties. Research supplement. *British Journal of Special Education,* Vol. 16, No. 4.

Wolfendale, S. (1983) *Parental Participation in Children's Development and Education.* London: Gordon & Breach.

Wolfendale, S. (1988) *The Parental Contribution to Assessment.* Developing Horizons No. 10. Stratford-upon-Avon, National Council for Special Education (now National Association for Special Educational Needs).

Wolfendale, S. (ed.) (1989) *Parental Involvement: Developing Networks between Home, School and Community.* London: Cassell.

Wolfendale, S. (1992) *Primary Schools and Special Needs: Policy, Planning and Provision.* 2nd edition. London: Cassell.

Wolfendale, S. and Bryans, T. (1979) *Identification of Learning Difficulties: A Model for Intervention.* Stafford: National Association of

Remedial Education (now National Association for Special Educational Needs).

Wolfendale, S., Bryans, T., Fox, M., Labram, A. and Sigston, A. (eds) (1992) *The Profession and Practice of Educational Psychology.* London: Cassell.

Wolfendale, S., Harskamp, A., Labram, A. and Millward, I. (1990) Governors and special educational needs: a collaborative inservice training programme. *Educational and Child Psychology*, Vol. 7, No. 2, pp. 46–54.

Woodhead, M. (1991) Psychology and the cultural construction of 'children's needs'. Chapter 3 in M. Woodhead, P. Light and R. Carr (eds), *Growing Up in a Changing Society*. London: Routledge and Open University Press.

ADDRESSES

MENCAP, 115 Golden Lane, London EC 1Y 0TJ.

81 NETWORK, 52 Magnaville Road, Bishop's Stortford, Herts. CM23 4DW.

Newham Parents' Centre, 747 Barking Road, London E13 9ER.

PIP (Parents in Partnership), Top Portakabin, Clare House, St George's Hospital, Blackshaw Road, London SW17 0QT.

SNAP (Special Needs Advisory Project) MENCAP/Spastics Society in Wales, 169 City Road, Cardiff CF2 3JB.

CHAPTER 8

Emerging initiatives in parental involvement and home–school links

CHAPTER OVERVIEW

Practice over the last few years has provided the impetus for the emerging developments described in this chapter. They include: consultation with parents; judging school performance by its parental involvement activities as one of the indices of effectiveness; the idea of a home–school agreement; and the scope and limitations of the parents' charters.

EMERGING INITIATIVES: ENSURING EFFECTIVE PRACTICE?

A number of factors set the initiatives described in this chapter apart from other developments in parental involvement outlined in this book and others:

- Their genesis undoubtedly lies in earlier and now-established practice, although they are distinctively different.
- Each is derived from or influenced in some way by the advent of the 1988 Education Reform Act.
- Each broadens the scope from parent as educator to parent as participant in education processes, though 'partnership' is not made explicit in all.

These initiatives are described as 'emerging' because none of them is (yet?) in evidence routinely in a significant number of schools. They are either the result of projects (parent consultation, home–school agreement), an idea under consideration (parental involvement as a performance indicator) or politically inspired (parents' charters). So we cannot know whether or not they are or could be 'good' practice. However, each merits serious attention; each has its own rationale – and each is sufficiently rooted in reality for us to consider how effective it might be in operation, routinely, in schools. Besides this, at a time when notions of accountability and quality assurance are being included in appraisal of school 'performance', it behoves us to consider whether these particular initiatives could make a *positive* contribution.

Related key concepts are ones explored in earlier chapters, most notably issues of *rights*, *entitlement* and *responsibilities*. The key concepts for this chapter are embedded in the very names of the initiatives described; that is,

---

CONSULTATION WITH PARENTS

PARENTAL INVOLVEMENT AS AN *INDICATOR*

HOME–SCHOOL *AGREEMENT*

PARENTS' *CHARTERS*

For each of these developments, a progression is denoted from education-initiated work through to politically inspired plans and recommendations, which could form the basis for further legislation. There is not much literature on these issues, by definition – these are burgeoning developments, yet to be enshrined in textbooks. What literature I have come across is mentioned in the chapter.

CONSULTATION WITH PARENTS

The premise behind consultation with parents is that it is a good idea to ask parents what they think about the school their children attend. While this is beautifully simple as a premise, translation into reality with no historical precedent of course takes considerable hard work and commitment.

The starting point, as Abbott *et al.* (1989) claim, is that 'every parent has a positive interest in, and expectations of, the school which their child attends' (p. 3). Indeed, this premise lay at the heart of the projects that Abbott and colleagues describe, which are essentially about school review processes, but which included the parental perspective as a key element. Their fundamental principle was that 'parents are the third part of the triangle – teachers, pupils, parents' (p. 3). Reflecting a contemporary view of parent as consumer, they go on to state:

parents may be regarded as the customers or clients, and a school like other organisations must strive to satisfy their customers/clients, and provide regular opportunities for parents to comment on their level of satisfaction with what the school offers. (p. 4)

The authors are realistic enough to proffer a list of problems arising from involving parents in school-based review (p. 25), but suggest, on the basis of the project which they initiated, that all or some of these may be surmountable. The existence of obstacles, such as reconciling disparate views of parents and teachers, reaching an adequate number of representative parents, and ensuring that an articulate, confident parent lobby does not preclude the voice of other parents being heard and heeded, should not deter schools from carrying out the exercise.

The model of consultation aims to go beyond the school-dominated presentation of its affairs to a participation that promotes joint 'ownership' of the issues uncovered – to shared celebration of achievements and collective responsibility for the solving of problems. Basing their suggestions on the project, in which a number of primary and secondary schools consulted parents and reported upon their findings, Abbott *et al*. offer a range of possible consultation strategies (see p. 26):

1 use of questionnaire – for all parents or a random sample;
2 conducting structured interviews;
3 holding open-forum meetings where parents are invited to contribute to an agenda for open discussion;
4 teachers collecting parental views on selected topics at parent consultation sessions or open evenings;
5 teachers and governors working together to obtain parents' views on given topics.

Hargreaves *et al*. (1989) provide a case study in their guideline booklet *Planning for School Development*, illustrating how parents were consulted on the pupils' performance in reading, a particular area of concern in the secondary school concerned. Indeed, the head had received a number of complaints from parents about their children's reading levels. So as part of data collection from various sources, the views of parents were solicited at a language workshop. A number of targets were subsequently set, with inbuilt success criteria, including increased involvement of support staff and parents in pupils' reading development. In the shorter term, the review teams were able to report a modest improvement in enlisting the assistance of parents and support staff.

Barrell (1990) likewise reports upon an exercise in parent consultation, acknowledges and describes 'teething troubles' and problem-solving attempts, and concludes,

there is now much evidence to show that, although it took some time to establish appropriate aims and some aspects are yet to become established, the scheme has been held in high regard by teachers, parents and children and most have benefited greatly from the experiences involved.

On a different but related tack, the principle of 'consultation' can be extended to the traditional parent–teacher exchange of information about individual children's progress (and see Chapter 6). This is a dialogue on supposedly equal terms between teacher and parent (and sometimes child), but it has the potential to realize in practice a fuller exchange of views, which can lead to action based on a consultation, rather than simply information-give, model.

Several American writers favour a more dynamic, action-focused mode of exchange known as the parent–teacher conference, which takes the British-style open evening further by encouraging parents and teachers to prepare carefully, and by providing a range of strategies for improving listening and question-asking skills, and negotiating and agreeing learning and behaviour-change goals. Mcloughlin (1987) sees recent moves in America towards the 'conferencing' approach as being driven by some extent by the parent-empowering movement, and, to return to the consultation model espoused by Abbott *et al.*, an essential ingredient is information sharing, with the purpose of leading to action seen to benefit all parties. Negative, critical views can be expressed within a supportive framework, instead of being suppressed or leaking out through covert means. For positive feedback from parents to teachers and vice versa, the consultative model provides a viable forum.

PARENTAL INVOLVEMENT AS A PERFORMANCE INDICATOR

It was during 1989 that it was suggested that one index of a school's effectiveness could be the extent and type of its involvement of parents. The main perpetrator of this proposal was the government, via what was then the Department of Education and Science, and one of the prime sources was a speech by one of the then Ministers of State at the DES, Angela Rumbold. Circulated as a press release, this was *Development of Performance Indicators: Key to Effective Management* (DES, 1989). It referred to a small, select pilot exercise which had taken place in forty primary and secondary schools within eight local education authorities. For the purposes of this chapter, only the parental involvement performance indicator will be referred to.

The kinds of index of parental involvement schools could be judged by include:

* communication with parents, verbal and written;
* objectives for parental involvement;
* activities denoting active parental participation;

111

- responsibilities the school wants or expects parents to assume;
- statistical data concerning parental choice of the school.

A performance indicator can be defined as an item of information collected at regular intervals in order to track the performance of a system (Fitz-Gibbon, 1990). An 'item of information' can include 'hard' data such as examination results (one sort of outcome of school effectiveness) or 'soft' data such as the report of an attitude survey which purports to reflect the status quo. An example of the latter for our purposes could be the results of a questionnaire asking parents if they feel the school actively welcomes them, provides them with the requisite information and involves them in activities. In this way the consultation model described above could form part of a performance indicator system. Because 'performance indicators' is such a fluid concept in education, certainly at the time of writing, it is possible to explore what potential it might have, and more to the point how it could benefit the entire school community, given that that comprises teachers, non-teaching staff, pupils, parents and governors.

A minimalist approach could be for the school to work out (preferably with parents) a list of activities it currently engages in (the current parental involvement indicators), together with a list of prospective activities (goals and future indicators). Outcomes as they occur could be marked off or recorded against the items on each list, which could be always available. In this way a school's performance would always be open and accountable.

A more ambitious, maximalist approach could be to list items, each of which lead to performance statements – a fuller, elaborated version of the minimalist approach, in that each item descriptor contains an outline of methods by which current and future activities have been and could be achieved, and against which the effectiveness of a range of methods could be evaluated. Thus quality control could be built into appraisal of school effectiveness.

The government intends that, under the arrangements for school inspection as specified in the Education (Schools) Act 1992, inspection teams shall (a) heed the views of parents and (b) appraise the extent of a school's parental and community involvement as key indicators.

HOME–SCHOOL AGREEMENT

Alternative but, as we shall see, not synonymous terms are 'contract' and 'concordat'. The heart of an *agreement* is a signed undertaking by teachers (the school) and parents as to relative responsibilities, which constitutes a pledge to achieve these, though not necessarily means of redress. A concept of *rights* and *entitlement* underlies such statements of mutual intent.

An early version of this idea was the Parents' Charter produced during the 1980s by the Campaign for the Advancement of State Education. According to a CASE spokesperson (in a personal communication), that original list is now defunct, superseded by later events. However, it is worth drawing attention to it as an early exemplar of a statement of rights. It sets out a list of what parents could and should expect from schools, such as a welcome, invitations to visit school and regular information, and sets these within the broader framework of what parents could expect from the LEA as the overall provider of education.

Macbeth (1989) refers to an earlier publication of his in which he outlines the thinking behind and substance of a 'signed understanding'. In this conception a declaration signed by parents provides for a guarantee of co-operation by them with school, and Macbeth (1989) suggests sanctions for non-compliance, such as denying a place at a given school for the child of non-co-operating parents. Macbeth is the first to acknowledge that the idea of a signed understanding along these lines is 'a leap into the unknown and may, for that reason, be unappealing at this stage' (p. 26). However, he envisages a minority of uncooperative parents, and the broader framework to the signed understanding is a 'minimum programme of parent–teacher liaison' which contains twelve pointers towards positive and effective co-operation. Widlake points out (1986) that such a 'concordat' could keep the power balance in the hands of teachers, but he sees potential in this idea of a signed declaration provided we build in *rights* as integral, as well as *duties*.

In parallel with these publications came a discussion paper from the National Association of Head Teachers (1988), defining and describing a home–school contract of partnership. This model would:

- set out the expectations which schools and parents would have of each other;
- require schools and parents to commit themselves to obligations and responsibilities implied by these expectations.

It is a two-way written agreement, with one column headed 'pupil and parent expectations of the school' and the other entitled 'school's expectations of parents and pupils'.

There are those who baulk at the idea behind a 'contract', who feel that it stiffens and formalizes the home–school relationship to such an extent that it might militate against the very entity that it seeks to promote, namely, a harmonious partnership. Critics also point out that unless there are means of redress (and does this mean litigation, ultimately?) a *contract* is ineffective. However, it seems in practice that a contract or agreement could have much to commend it, in articulating the 'nuts and bolts' of parental involvement, setting out the rights and responsibilities of all parties, and providing a supportive framework for the enactment of home–school links. In fact, the NAHT is a partner, with the RSA, in a wide-ranging project exploring the feasibility of a contract/agreement, the 'Home/School Contract of Partnership Project' (see RSA in addresses at end of chapter). This extract from one of the project newsletters describes its scope and purpose:

> it sets out to identify and develop ways of establishing more open and equal relationships between school and the home, recognising both shared goals and complementary roles for teachers and parents. The Project aims to identify replicable models for developing home–school relationships, and to use these in dialogue with other countries in the EC in order to find ways to provide a more active and integrated role for parents and the home, in the education and training of young people.

Thus the scope is broader than the narrower definition of contract/agreement might imply, as the work of the project schools shows (Jones *et al.*, 1992).

Tomlinson (1991) reviews the short history of the contract/agreement idea in certain European countries including the UK, and provides a couple of examples as well as a model *educational agreement*, a variant of previous ones, which could be used as a starting point for schools. This is three-way, comprising statements of intent to co-operate on the part of parents, teachers and pupils, and would not have legal force but would be 'binding in honour only' (that is, not a legal document but recognized and taken into account in law). Before the 1992 general election, the Labour Party was committed to 'the parents' right to a home/school partnership agreement' (Labour Party, 1991). This document contains a model home–school partnership agreement which was put forward as a 'best practice' composite of such agreements currently in use. The Conservative government preferred to utilize the medium of a universally available 'statement' in its Parent's Charter to convey messages about rights and responsibilities.

For all schools to embrace the idea of a 'signed understanding' would signal commitment, reinforce the idea that 'involvement' is a two-way process (notions of mutuality and reciprocity; see Chapters 1 and 2) and that *rights* and *responsibilities* are different sides of the one coin, and ultimately should be a guarantee of children's best interests.

THE PARENTS' CHARTERS

We come now to the most explicitly political of the 'new', emerging ideas. Irrespective of political origin, the overarching philosophy behind declarations in the public domain such as the Conservative Party's Citizen's Charter and Parent's Charter and the Labour Party's

Parents' Charter was to appeal to the voting public and convince it that the party in question had the public interest truly at heart.

Reflecting their parent documents, the citizens' charters of both main parties, the parents' charters offered a number of promises and guarantees to parents for high-quality education which rest upon a foundation of rights and entitlements. Let us sketch the contents of each.

The Labour Party's The Parents' Charter

A short introduction sets out the underlying principles of *partnership*, followed by the bulk of the document, the enumeration of ten rights:

1 parents' right to know – the right to LEA and school information;
2 parents' right to information about schools' performance – instead of 'league tables' (see below) a new Education Standards Commission is proposed to moderate and monitor assessment results at local and national levels;
3 parents' right of access to the teaching staff, with arrangements rather more flexible than the traditional open evening, and including a regular 'teachers' surgery';
4 parents' right to a record of their child's achievements, as part of a national, statutory Record of Achievement scheme;
5 parents' right to participate, and to encourage participation through a national framework;
6 parents' right to advice, through, for example, education advice centres (and see Ray Phillips's case study in Chapter 10);
7 parents' right to action; for example, to complain, via local mechanisms set up for the purpose;
8 parents' right to a hearing for possibly contentious issues; for example, proposed closure of a school;
9 parents' right to open government – the right to be consulted and kept informed on issues;
10 parents' right to a home–school partnership agreement (see discussion above), a model of which is given in an appendix.

The Conservative Government/DES The Parent's Charter—You and Your Child's Education: Raising the Standard

This is a glossy, illustrated A5-format booklet, issued in September 1991. Two fundamental rights are put forward: 'The Right to Know' and 'The Right to Choose', under each of which are a number of statements and promises. The areas of proposed legislation (for the 1991–2 parliamentary session) were in red type (now incorporated into the Education (Schools) Act 1992).

Five key documents were promised under 'The Right to Know':

1   a report about your child – already promised under the Education Reform Act, but elaborated and extended to embrace curriculum, assessment and general progress;
2   regular reports from independent inspectors, who in turn will be subject to being checked by a residual number of Her Majesty's Inspectors (HMI) at the DES;
3   performance tables for all local schools (these are the 'league tables' referred to earlier);
4   a prospectus or brochure about each school (as is already the case);
5   an annual report from your school's governors (a current requirement; but it will be extended to include information about standards achieved, attendance and school-leavers' destinations).

Under 'The Right to Choose' parents were reminded about: their children's right to a free education; grant-maintained schools and City Technology Colleges; their right to say which school they prefer and open enrolment; choices post-16; and the obligation on local education authorities to publish information as to how they provide for children with special educational needs.

Finally, there was information as to 'your child's right to a good education' and 'what to do if things go wrong', accompanied by a number of examples of issues and parental concerns. The booklet ends with a reiteration of what 'active partnership' means in practice.

Reaction and responses: a diversity of views

Both parents' charters received a considerable press in 1991, though naturally the Conservative government/DES Parent's Charter attracted most attention, not only because it was that of the government of the day, and not only because legislation was promised on some of the ideas, but because several of these ideas represent a departure from established practice and bring the notion of consumerism to the heart of education. Whereas the Labour Party parents' charter placed an emphasis on *empowerment* and *participation*, the government stresses parents' rights to choice of educational goods and services. The political consensus area is that of 'the right to information', but the differences of degree and emphasis are profound, though both charters professed a commitment to quality education.

The furore surrounding the most contentious proposals reflects debate and disagreement about the best ways of achieving quality education. The proposals that provoked ire from teachers' unions, parents' associations and professional organizations have been the idea of 'league tables', independent inspection and the dismantling in its present form of Her Majesty's Inspectorate. Criticisms included:

- The Parent's Charter (DES) is long on rhetoric but short on resources.
- Independent inspection is no guarantee of impartiality and excellence of judgement.
- A league table approach is invidious, superficial and mis-leading.
- What national overview of maintenance of standards can there be with an HMI with a diminished role?

On the last point, Saunders and Rigg (1991) express concern that, in a consumerist model, no one has any overriding interest in maintaining a sense of equity, and the national interest is consequently put at risk.

We need to distinguish between the *idea* of a charter (expression and guarantee of rights) and the content. We might endorse the principle of a charter, but acknowledge that in reality it is bound to be contentious; that is, to offend the status quo if it contains ideas for change. The alternative is to have a bland set of statements that offer little or no protection.

The ideas in this chapter offer some promise for parents to be part of the education process, and go further than a number of parental involvement approaches described in earlier chapters. Each of the four areas of 'emerging initiatives' in this chapter contains potential for parents to judge quality and school effectiveness on the basis of first-hand information and participation. There may not be a 'best buy' among these ideas; rather, an amalgam on offer to parents might be an effective guarantee for involvement on equal terms.

EXERCISE: Examining your attitudes to these emerging initiatives

Purpose: The emerging initiatives described in this chapter are not routinely part of the majority of schools. Having the opportunity to think about their advantages and disadvantages could be a preparation for you to initiate one or more of these ideas when you have the opportunity. At least you can clarify your attitudes to them.

What to do: With respect to each of the major ideas outlined in this chapter – that is:

* consultation with parents;
* parental involvement as a performance indicator;
* home–school agreement;
* parents' charter;

please complete a questionnaire like the one overleaf.

Major idea . . . .
1   The idea attracts me.   Yes/No

    If *Yes*, say why . . . .

    If *No*, say why . . . .

2   This idea is practical and possible.   Yes/No

    If *Yes*, say how . . . .

    If *No*, say why not . . . .

3   This idea will give parents more say in education.   Yes/No

    If *Yes*, explain how . . . .

    If *No*, explain why not . . . .

4   This idea will also give teachers more say in education.   Yes/No

    If *Yes*, explain how . . . .

    If *No*, explain why not . . . .

5   This idea will encourage more partnership with parents.   Yes/No

    If Yes, say why . . . .

    If No, say why not . . . .

Comments: At most this questionnaire can be completed four
times, for each of the major ideas. It can be completed on your own,
then discussed in a group.

CHAPTER SUMMARY

**Four major 'emerging initiatives' in parental involvement have been
presented, with reference to what little literature and evidence there
is currently available. There seems considerable potential in parental consultation, parental involvement as a performance indicator,
home–school agreement and a parents' charter. The political ramifica-**

tions of the ideas have been noted, and readers have been invited to consider the feasibility of each of the ideas from their own perspective.

REFERENCES

Since this is an embryonic area there are no special or seminal texts yet available, so it is suggested that readers pick and choose from the list below.

Abbott, R., Birchenough, M. and Steadman, S. (1989) *External Perspectives on School-based Review*. York: Longman.

Barrell, N. (1990) *Managing Consultations in a Middle School to Involve Parents and Children in Target Setting*. Paper given at annual conference of BEMAS, September. Contact Hampshire LEA.

DES (1989) Development of Performance Indicators: Key to Effective Management. Speech given by Minister Angela Rumbold, 5 December.

DES (1991) *The Parent's Charter*. London: DES.

Fitz-Gibbon, C. (ed.) (1990) *Performance Indicators*. BERA Dialogues, No. 2. Clevedon: Multilingual Matters.

Hargreaves, D., Hopkins, D., Leask, M., Connolly, J. and Robinson, P. (1989) *Planning for School Development: Advice to Governors, Headteachers and Teachers*. London: DES.

Jones, G., Bastiani, J., Bell, G. and Chapman, C. (1992) *A Willing Partnership* (final report, January). London: Royal Society of Arts.

Labour Party (1991) *The Parents' Charter*. London: The Labour Party.

Macbeth, A. (1989) *Involving Parents*. London: Heinemann.

Mcloughlin, C. (1987) *Parent–Teacher Conferencing*. Springfield, Ill: Charles C. Thomas.

National Association of Head Teachers (NAHT) (1988) *Home–School Contract of Partnership: A Discussion Paper*. Haywards Health: NAHT.

Saunders, L. and Rigg, M. (1991) Article on educational choice. *Consumer Policy Review*, October.

Tomlinson, S. (1991) Teachers and parents: home–school partnerships. In *Education and Training Paper No. 7*. London: Institute for Public Policy Research.

Widlake, P. (1986) *Reducing Educational Disadvantage*. Milton Keynes: Open University Press.

ADDRESSES

The Labour Party, 150 Walworth Road, London SE17 1JT.
National Association of Head Teachers (NAHT), 1 Heath Square, Boltro Road, Haywards Heath, West Sussex RH16 1 BL.
Royal Society of Arts (RSA), 8 John Adam Street, London WC2N 6 EZ.

CHAPTER 9

Participation by parents in education: prospects and predictions

CHAPTER OVERVIEW

This chapter draws together a number of the topics, themes and issues dealt with in previous chapters. In that respect it is a summary, but it serves two additional purposes: it comprises a stocktaking exercise as to where we are in the realm of parental involvement, and enables us to make a number of tentative predictions concerning future directions. The chapter also provides a prelude to Chapters 10 and 11, the case studies which epitomize and illustrate contemporary practice. Several key aspects will be looked at in this chapter which have a bearing upon emerging and future directions, namely parental involvement/ partnership models and policies.

SURVEYING THE SCENE

This section will comprise the main part of the chapter and could be subtitled 'From macro to micro', since it will first survey a number of trends at national level, then focus on the local level. In turn, this will lead to scrutiny of the school as a discrete community. It is evident, but perhaps needs stating explicitly, that each and every initiative interconnects not only within a level but between levels. For example, a school-based or school-initiated venture relies on local education authority backing and support; in turn, an LEA initiative will reflect some kind of broader consensus, if not the spirit of the times. In fact, the greater the degree of interconnectedness, the greater is the likelihood of successful maintenance of the initiative, since coalitions of interest and commitment are powerful guarantees. We will look at the idea of 'collective responsibility' later in the chapter.

The national trend

Throughout the book there has been reference to small- and larger-scale developments and events which can be construed as providing evidence for trends. Currently a number of sources provide a diverse range of evidence for movement at national level, which indicate that there has been and continues to be a significant shift towards increasing parental involvement, and in some quarters a realignment in the power balance, towards an approximation of power-sharing. A number of these sources are now commented on.

Legislation

In Chapter 2 and other chapters (see, for example, Chapter 7), we saw how recent educational legislation as well as the 1989 Children Act confers rights on and reiterates responsibilities of parents, no less than for professionals who work with or on behalf of children. Enumeration of rights and responsibilities provides an entrée into decision-making at a number of levels; for example, parents as governors, parental involvement in assessment, and parents' right to receive information about schools and their assessment results (see Chapter 8).

Survey evidence

Chapter 2 referred to the national research carried out by Jowett *et al.* (1991) as well as the HMI (1991) survey into the incidence and range of parental involvement initiatives in a sample of local education authorities. 'Proof positive' is provided by these means of increasing home–school links and commensurately a shift in attitude, by teachers in particular, towards acceptance of parental involvement as a positive force on behalf of children.

Projects and networking

Projects have been referred to in the book on innumerable occasions. Many are discrete and localized, and not necessarily capable of being generalized. However, there are notable initiatives operating across the UK to the extent of constituting a 'critical mass', which are therefore worthy of being described as 'national' and so provide further evidence of an identified trend. *Portage*, described in Chapter 7, is one such, and the NAHT/RSA project into the *home/school contract of partnership* mentioned in Chapter 8 is another. A key feature of this is the links being set up between project schools, which constitute effective networking. One current venture is the setting up of a UK Directory of home–school initiatives (National Home–School Development Group; see addresses at end of chapter).

One prediction is that there will gradually be increased contact with similar groupings in the rest of Europe, as the single market will facilitate the links which are already, albeit on a small scale, beginning to happen; for example, as part of the NAHT/RSA project.

Evidence at LEA level

An earlier publication (Wolfendale, 1987) sought to provide some evidence of commitment to and backing of parental involvement by LEAs. The second edition of this book, published in 1992, amends this table, as it was realized that LEA commitment is variable and vulnerable, both to financial cutbacks and to a dearth of funds for development work. Regrettably, a current example of such a constraint is the Oxfordshire parental involvement programme, which was curtailed during 1991 for lack of funding. Over recent years, however, there has been plenty of evidence of LEA support for ventures such as adoption of PACT (home–school reading) and IMPACT (home–school maths) as well as Portage. A small number of LEAs have been pace-setters, with Coventry as the leading LEA in this area for the range, depth and sustained nature of its initiatives.

The four case studies in Chapter 10 epitomize process, product and, certainly to date, a demonstrable commitment by the LEA. There is no shortage of advice on how LEAs can initiate and maintain parental involvement/partnership programmes (Brighouse, 1985). Bastiani (1989) envisages a role for LEAs which suggests: a tailoring of national policies and trends to local needs and circumstances; support and backing for school-based work, consisting of resources as well as personnel; provision of in-service opportunities in the area; teacher release to pursue home–school tasks; and creation of a 'mediation service' to provide information and advice, together with conciliation facilities to deal with disputes. This is similar to the Labour Party's idea of an Education Advice Centre, a concept realized in practice by the Newham Parents' Centre (see case study by Ray Phillips, Chapter 10).

A tentative prediction at this point is that as LEA power continues to wane, devolution could lead to fragmentation and dissipation of good practice. Opportunities for networking and sharing of experiences will be reduced in an educational climate where competition overrides co-operation. After all, publication of school results (see previous chapter), while fulfilling a criterion of accountability to parents, cannot help but foster rivalry between schools, which might be inimical to the spirit of partnership between teachers and with parents.

The view from schools

The school level is the paramount one and effective implementation of home–school initiatives has to be the *raison d'être* of policies at LEA and national levels. There are thousands of examples of effective parent–teacher co-operation up and down the land which collectively constitute the evidence. Of those, a minority are described in books, articles and reports, but most remain unreported, unheralded, and celebrated only by the participants themselves.

From this experience much has been learned. For example, we have learned first hand that process is as important as outcomes and that the area of parental involvement has to be accorded high priority and given a high profile if any school-based initiative is to succeed; that is, to take off and be maintained over a period of time. Over time, too, we have gained a perspective on the key requisites for effective co-operative ventures. A number of features emerge which represent part of our collective experience to date, and which will be looked at now. Their significance is that each is rooted in first-hand experience; forms part of 'lessons learned' (positive as well as negative experience); can be conceptualized abstractly as well as operationalized in action, as has been the case; and provides pointers towards future effective practice.

Whole-school policy on parental participation

Parental involvement practice has generally started discretely, often at the instigation of individual teachers, who were perhaps inspired by an in-service presentation or an article about practice elsewhere. The idea of *policy* usually arises as practice establishes itself, as needs are identified and as commitment emerges (there is a parallel here with the area of equal opportunities; see Chapter 7).

Accumulated wisdom from the hard-won experience of all participants (researchers, practitioners and parents) leads inescapably to the conclusion that a whole-school policy represents a statement of principle; an affirmation of commitment; the sum of experience in that setting to date; and an enumeration of goals and of the means by which these can be achieved. From their research Jowett *et al.* (1991) aver that, rather than being a peripheral extra or optional activity, work with parents should be viewed as an integral part of the way schools function, and that it needs to become a key element in the school system. Other writers, drawing on their own as well as others' experience, have concluded that policy formation and adoption is an inescapable and necessary underpinning of activities. Those authors who have put forward detailed policy recommendations include Wolfendale (1983), Macbeth (1989) and Bastiani (1989). Wolfendale's rest upon a set of principles (Chapter 10) and Macbeth's upon twelve points – his 'policy steps' (p. 176) – while Bastiani's book deals entirely with implementation of a whole-school approach. Professional associations too have endorsed the idea of policy formulation and adoption (NUT, 1987; NARE, 1988).

There are schools with written policies on parental involvement (see the school case studies in Chapter 11). On the basis of evidence, it is predicted that, notwithstanding the changing climate referred to above, an increasing number of schools will adopt a parental involvement policy, which is both a symbolic announcement of solidarity between home and school and a programme for action. To borrow a business-originated phrase, a policy is a mission statement – a public proclamation of intent.

Parental involvement as a reflector of the ethos of the school

The 'culture' of any school rests upon and is composed of a host of attitudes and philosophies. If these are coherent, we can describe the prevailing culture ('ethos' and 'climate' are alternative words describing the same concept), albeit in rather vague, qualitative, impressionistic terms. Usually the more discordant and discrepant within-school attitudes and philosophies are, the less it is possible to describe the culture, even 'character', of a school.

Pollard (1985) refers to 'institutional bias', which defines the prevailing ethos of any one school, and points to parental involvement as one area where between-school differences show. An equally *social* (though differently cast) view of school and learning is expressed by Kutnick (1988), who promotes the view that teachers need to reappraise and broaden their conception of learning to embrace parental participation as a legitimate part of the social and learning climate of the school.

The view that school as an *institution* is a powerful source of support for children and families brings us full circle, to the rationales underlying many of the compensatory intervention programmes referred to in Chapter 2 (for earlier expositions on policies to alleviate disadvantage see Field, 1977; Mortimore and Blackstone, 1982). In a text published at the time of maximum post-Plowden educational priority areas programmes, many of which promoted parental participation, Sharp and Green (1975) dug deep into the constructions of school by parents. As sociologists they acknowledge that their methods, common to most other social scientists, 'only capture the surface character of the interaction' and therefore it is difficult 'to come to grips with the underlying nature of the social totality in which parents and teachers are embedded' (p. 211). The reality of discordant, discrepant views, competing values and misunderstandings of intent is addressed by Bastiani (1990), who in effect urges participants to engage in honest dialogue to explore each other's expectations and attitudes. Such a process, he suggests, will require organizational changes in the school, and he offers 'ten commandments' by which consensus and partnership can eventually be achieved. Haynes *et al.* (1988) also offer suggestions for the enhancement of the school climate through parental involvement – again, this involves changes at organizational level in addition to discrete action by individual teachers and groups of parents.

A prediction here might be that schools will be forced by the advent of a parents' charter (see Chapter 8) and the ensuing legislation to adopt pervasive and corporate strategies to promote parental participation.

Parental involvement as an indication of the effectiveness of the school

Inclusion of parental involvement policies could be taken as one of the ways in which school performance can be judged. Parental involvement as a possible performance indicator was discussed in Chapter 8 as one of the emerging initiatives, and is enshrined in the Education (Schools) Act 1992.

Mortimore (1989) describes the junior school Project in which he was one of the researchers (reported in Mortimore *et al.*, 1988), which came up with twelve key factors for effective (junior) schooling, one of which is parental involvement at a number of levels of school life. Openness and accessibility were paramount, and Mortimore sums up in these words: 'our findings show parental involvement in the life of the school to be a positive influence upon pupils' progress and development' (p. 171).

Although it seems straightforward that parental involvement could constitute one index of a school's effectiveness, nevertheless there are inherent difficulties in setting out markers of this kind in the current era of decentralization. Reynolds (1991) identifies the paradox whereby a basically constructive way of looking at schools' functioning and effectiveness should at the same time increase competitiveness between schools, as parents and others use these indices as a guide by which to compare and contrast schools. This of course is the underlying philosophy of the Education Reform Act and subsequent legislation, based on the grounds that quality is better assured when consumers have real choice.

Reynolds foresees many new tasks being imposed upon schools as part of the increased public scrutiny. The prediction here is that parental involvement as an indicator will prove to be a mixed blessing, for the reasons just stated and touched upon in previous chapters.

AN ECOLOGICAL PERSPECTIVE AS AN EXPRESSION OF COLLECTIVE RESPONSIBILITY AND PARTNERSHIP WITH PARENTS

The broader sociological dimension identified above as an essential corollary to appraising parental involvement leads inescapably to an overarching perspective that embraces sociological and psycho-educational constructs – that is, the ecological perspective. A seminal influence upon the 'ecological way of thinking' is acknowledged to be Bronfenbrenner (1979), who viewed 'ecological intervention' as a way of analysing children's situations. This involves appraising the total sum of influences on children in their environment and, reciprocally, their interactions and the ways in which they impinge on people and situations. A number of writers describe ecological approaches to education: for example, Wolfendale (1992, Appendix 5) outlines practical steps for eco-mapping children's environments, and Thomas (1991) provides a theoretical review of the area and discusses the implications for practice. Vetere and Gale (1987; and see Chapter 3) demonstrate empirically such an approach applied to scrutiny of family life. Ashman and Elkins (1990) sum up the rationale: 'the ecological perspective . . . views the developing person in the context of family, neighbourhood, community and societal system' (pp. 400–1).

Ian Walker (see addresses at end of chapter) describes the application of the ecological perspective to a typology he is currently developing to explore parental involvement in literacy practices. The five levels of his typology are:

1   no parent involvement;
2   parents as clients;
3   parents as supporters;
4   towards an ecological perspective;
5   an ecological perspective.

Level 5 is evidently the fullest expression of parental participation in literacy practices. (For this information the author is indebted to personal communication.)

This holistic view of parental participation raises questions about collective responsibility. It would seem to be an integral part of such a view that participants are equally involved and share corporate responsibility. In turn this brings us back to *partnership*, one of the key concepts examined in Chapter 2, where a number of characteristics defining partnership were presented. Inherent in such a concept is of course power-sharing, brought about where it did not previously exist by processes of *empowerment*. Sayer (1989) cautions that 'it is one thing to subscribe to principles of partnership . . . what is less easy to define is responsibility for making the partnership work' (p. 54).

We reach, once more, the political dimension of the debate and raise again the question of whether recent legislation encourages power-sharing or maintains the control in institutions (schools, and local education authorities if they continue in their present or even an amended form) vested explicitly in key people within them. It has already been pointed out that *rights* (as set out in the Citizen's Charter, the Parent's Charter and the Patient's Charter, for example) do not necessarily imply or lead to *equality* within decision-making. The balance of power in societal terms was examined by David (1980), and although her examination predated the 1988 Education Reform Act by nearly a decade, nevertheless, re-reading it in the contemporary context shows that her main messages still ring as true today. She argues for full parental participation in educational decision-making as well as corporate and collective responsibility on the part of the state, its institutions and the people for whom the services are supposed to be designed.

It is difficult to avoid a rather gloomy prediction that an ecological approach remains an attractive abstract concept and explanatory framework, but is unlikely to be taken on board by those already in positions of power and influence, and that those who remain unempowered will not easily have access to such models. As for the researchers and practitioners with their first-hand experience, hard-won insights and the necessary commitment, opportunity to apply ecology in practice in the future will remain limited without the requisite backing.

The major key concepts examined in this chapter are:

PARENTAL PARTICIPATION POLICY

PARENTAL INVOLVEMENT as reflector of the *ethos* of a school

PARENTAL INVOLVEMENT as indicator of school *effectiveness*

ECOLOGICAL PERSPECTIVE

COLLECTIVE RESPONSIBILITY

The reader is urged to look back to Chapter 1 at this point, to cross-refer to the key concepts introduced at that early point in the book, which have such a close correspondence with those examined in this chapter, namely:

| RIGHTS | EQUALITY | RECIPROCITY | EMPOWERMENT |

The key concepts presented in each chapter have been the abstract pegs on which discussion and example have hung. It is hoped that there has been an evident interrelationship between and among them.

TRAINING TEACHERS TO WORK WITH PARENTS

It was pointed out in Chapter 2 that the initial training phase was the most obvious and appropriate time for specific and targeted training in the requisite skills for working with other people, and especially parents. A number of exercises for developing communication skills with others were offered in Chapter 6.

Teachers are undeniably key facilitators, but we cannot take for granted equal competence in the sensitive area of human interaction among all teachers. In an area that Jowett *et al.* (1991) has described as 'complex and challenging', teachers from their initial training onwards are entitled to guidance and support in reappraising their attitudes; in developing communication skills; in understanding child-rearing and parenting practice; and in acquiring competence in the introduction and implementation of specific techniques (for example, in the home-based reading and mathematics area, or parental involvement in assessment). All this in addition to the current load upon teachers and onus upon teacher trainers? The justification is philosophical as well as pedagogical: the whole of this book has been an attempt to provide the rationale as well as the evidence to back up an ideological view that the future lies in closer home–school links, expressed by all the diverse means described in this and other books.

This conclusion – that teachers in training as well as serving teachers need training and support to work effectively in the area of parental involvement – has also been reached in other quarters. For example, OMEP (The World Organization for Early Childhood Education) produced in 1990 a document, *Training for Work with Parents*, which was targeted at teachers and also other practitioners and practitioner-trainers who work with children. Its recommendations include training in personal development, interpersonal skills, knowledge relevant to early-years workers, and specific considerations for working with parents. It is worth quoting from the introduction to this booklet, since it emphasizes an empowering approach, not just the imposition of views and practices from practitioners on parents:

> The aim of working with parents is to encourage self-determination through interdependence both within the community and in relation to families and young children. The translation of this aim into practice

has a number of interconnecting strands: the encouraging of thought-ful parenting; helping the adults fulfil their own needs by developing awareness of the services available through the government and the local authority and to use and to participate in development of these services. (p. 8).

Another view of the potential of the training phase for encouraging teacher–parent links is expressed by Tomlinson (1991), who suggests a network of regional staff colleges created by mergers of teacher train-ing institutions. These colleges 'could also act as centres for parent education courses – either in house or on an outreach basis, providing a proper service of information and "education about education" to parents' (p. 6).

As predictions, these can be looked on positively – but whether they are idealistic or rooted in reality as far as the future of teacher training is concerned cannot at this point be determined.

ENDPOINT: FROM PRINCIPLES TO PRACTICE

This book has been predicated on principles of equality and rights, and the fundamental entitlement of all parents to have maximum access to and participation in education processes on behalf of their own chil-dren and, collectively, of all children. Pedagogical as well as philo-sophical reasons, backed where possible by research and practice findings, have been advanced. In the UK we have much to celebrate in terms of the advances made in the area of parental participation – and, too, more to learn and apply. The duties and responsibilities all adults have towards children can, in their interests, best be expressed by a *coalition* of all the significant adults in children's lives. Is there any more powerful way to give children their basic rights, wherever they live and whatever their lifestyle, than through a partnership between adults?

A summary exercise now follows, to provide an opportunity to draw together ideas and opinions.

EXERCISE: Holding a debate on parental involvement

Purpose: To marshal all ideas and examples brought together in this and other books; to examine critically the rationales for and intentions behind parental involvement initiatives; to provide an opportunity to present a defence of home–school links as well as a critique of the rationale, theory and research.

What to do: This exercise is of course best done in group form, with one person presenting and arguing for the proposition and one for the opposition, followed by discussion, then a vote on the central motion.

The motion for the debate could be: 'That parental involvement in education and the fostering of the home–school relationship is in the child's best interests.'

Comments: As readers will know, proposers and opposers of a motion do not have to believe in what they are arguing for! This exercise is suggested as an opportunity to engage in lively debate and air the issues as thoroughly as possible.

CHAPTER SUMMARY

The chapter has aimed to draw together principles and practice and to make some cautious predictions. In all, there are seven sets of predictions offered in the chapter and they comprise a mix of hopeful and pessimistic views about future directions within parental involvement. The areas about which predictions were made have been: national, LEA and school-based initiatives; whole-school policy; parental involvement as reflecting school ethos and as an indicator of school effectiveness; and the potential for applying ecological perspectives to parental involvement practice. Finally, implications for teacher training were looked at.

FURTHER READING

Three sources are singled out, each of which reflects a major section of this chapter:

Bastiani, J. (1989) *Working with Parents: A Whole-school Approach*. Windsor: NFER-Nelson. Ideas and strategies for implementing whole-school policies are presented, covering topics such as communication, INSET, parents in school, home–school agreements and reporting to parents.

David, M. (1980) *The State, the Family and Education*. London: Routledge. Although, as mentioned in the text of this chapter, this book predates major recent educational legislation, its central theme and message are still pertinent, as the book raises issues to do with collective responsibility for children, means of empowerment and the place of education in promoting child and family interests.

Tomlinson, S. (1991) Teachers and parents: home–school partnerships. In *Education and Training Paper No. 7*. London: Institute for Public Policy Research. This paper forms part of a pamphlet which also addresses future teacher training. The Tomlinson paper briefly reviews parental involvement in the UK and four other European countries, and proposes future strategies, including the home–school agreement.

REFERENCES

Ashman, A. and Elkins, J. (1990) *Educating Children with Special Needs*. Englewood Cliffs, NJ: Prentice-Hall.

Bastiani, J. (1989) *Working with Parents: A Whole-school Approach*. Windsor: NFER-Nelson.

Bastiani, J. (1990) Home–school partnership fallacy: a change of teachers' attitudes is all that is needed. Chapter 6 in B. O'Hagan (ed.), *The Charnwood Papers: Fallacies in Community Education*. Nottingham: Education Now Books.

Brighouse, T. (1985) Parents and the local education authority. In C. Cullingford (ed.), *Parents, Teachers and Schools*. London: Robert Royce.

Bronfenbrenner, U. (1979) *The Ecology of Human Development: Experiments by Nature and Design*. Cambridge, Mass.: Harvard University Press.

David, M. (1980) *The State, the Family and Education*. London: Routledge & Kegan Paul.

Field, F. (ed.) (1977) *Education and the Urban Crisis*. London: Routledge & Kegan Paul.

Haynes, N., Comer, J. and Hamilton-Lee, M. (1988) School climate enhancement through parental involvement. *Journal of School Psychology*, Vol. 27, pp. 87–90.

HMI (1991) *Parents and Schools: Aspects of Parental Involvement in Primary and Secondary Schools, 1989–90*. London: DES.

Jowett, S., Baginsky, M. and MacNeil, M. M. (1991) *Building Bridges: Parental Involvement in Schools*. Windsor: NFER-Nelson.

Kutnick, P. (1988) *Relationships in the Primary School Classroom*. London: Paul Chapman.

Macbeth, A. (1989) *Involving Parents: Effective Parent–Teacher Relations*. Oxford: Heinemann Educational.

Mortimore, J. and Blackstone, T. (1982) *Disadvantage and Education*. London: Heinemann Educational Books.

Mortimore, P. (1989) School matters. Chapter 3.6 in B. Moon, P. Murphy and J. Raynor (eds), *Policies for the Curriculum*. London: Hodder & Stoughton, in association with the Open University.

Mortimore, P., Sammons, P., Ecob, R. and Stoll, L. (1988) *School Matters: The Junior Years*. Salisbury: Open Books.

NARE (National Association for Remedial Education) (1988) *Parents as Partners*. Guidelines No. 7. Stafford: NARE.

NUT (National Union of Teachers) (1987) *Pupils, Teachers and Parents*. London: NUT.

OMEP (The World Organization for Early Childhood Education) *Training for Work with Parents*. A working group report. Bakewell: OMEP.

Pollard, A. (1985) *The Social World of the Primary School*. London: Cassell.

Reynolds, D. (1991) School effectiveness and school improvement in the 1990s: a commissioned review. *Association for Child Psychology and Psychiatry Newsletter*, Vol. 13, No. 2, pp. 5–10.

Sayer, J. (1989) *Managing Schools*. London: Hodder & Stoughton.

Sharp, R. and Green, A. (1975) *Education and Social Control: A Study in Progressive Primary Education*. London: Routledge & Kegan Paul.

Thomas, G. (1991) Ecological interventions. Chapter 4 in S. Wolfendale, T. Bryans, M. Fox, A. Labram and A. Sigston (eds), *The Profession and Practice of Educational Psychology: Future Directions*. London: Cassell.

Tomlinson, S. (1991) Teachers and parents: home–school partnerships. *Education and Training Paper No. 7*. London: Institute for Public Policy Research.

Vetere, A. and Gale, A. (1987) *Ecological Studies of Family Life*. Chichester: Wiley.

Wolfendale, S. (1983) *Parental Participation in Children's Development and Education*. London: Gordon & Breach.

Wolfendale, S. (1987) *Primary chools and Special Needs: Policy, Planning and Provision*. London: Cassell. 2nd edition 1992.

ADDRESSES

National Home–School Development Group: contact Dr John Bastiani, School of Education, University of Nottingham, University Park, Nottingham NG7 2RD.

National Association for Remedial Education (NARE), 2 Lichfield Street, Stafford ST17 4JX (now National Association for Special Educational Needs).

National Union of Teachers (NUT), Hamilton House, Mabledon Place, London WC1H 9ND.

Walker, I. School of Early Childhood and Primary Education, Monash University, Frankston Campus, McMahons Road, Frankston, Victoria 3199, Australia.

The World Organization for Early Childhood Education (OMEP), c/o Huntcliffe, Over Lane, Baslow, Bakewell, Derbyshire DE4 1RT.

Preface to Chapters 10 and 11

Chapters 10 and 11 comprise the case studies, eight accounts of LEA and school-based collaboration with parents.

During the writing of this book invitations were extended to the authors of the case studies, who were known to be actively involved in initiatives in their work-setting, to write a short account of that work. Each responded with enthusiasm, reportedly pleased to celebrate the effectiveness of home–school links and to share the information with a wider audience. I am delighted to be able to include these first-hand accounts of practice.

The eight writers were asked to describe the origins of their initiative, the processes of implementation, findings to date and plans for the future. The reader will see how these practice descriptions illuminate, in a vivid fashion, much of the discussion in earlier chapters, at the same time as providing first-hand testimony as to the 'nuts-and-bolts' effort and hard work required in setting up projects which have no precedent. The reader will also gain insight into the many issues, some already discussed in the book, which have had to be addressed by the participants in these eight accounts. Fundamental to any and all kinds of parental involvement venture are issues of commitment, empowerment, partnership, resourcing and maintenance.

Chapter 10 contains four accounts of parental involvement initiated at LEA level, each of which demonstrates commitment on the part of education committee members and officers in the education departments, as well as of teachers and parents. These represent a mix of top-down and bottom-up approaches. Parental involvement policies at LEA level are intended to be pervasive and permeating, and represent a particular ideology and commitment based on the rationale outlined in Chapter 2.

Chapter 11 focuses on school-based initiatives, which represent micro-application of these policies within individual settings. That no two schools are alike is a truism, but it is well exemplified in four very different accounts of the origins of and reasons for setting up and implementing a host of activities denoting involvement of or partnership with parents.

For teachers in training, their tutors, practitioners in schools and education departments, these case studies could be an inspiration, as they reflect emerging and effective practice.

CHAPTER 10

Case studies of parental participation in four local education authorities

CHAPTER OVERVIEW

The case studies are as follows:

- Humberside: Alwyn Morgan, School Community Officer, for Humberside LEA;
- Newham: Ray Phillips, Director, Newham Parents' Centre;
- Northumberland: Sue Miller, Educational Psychologist, Northumberland LEA, and Jean Robinson, Advisory Teacher, Northumberland LEA;
- Warwickshire: Ann Evans, Inspector, Warwickshire LEA.

HUMBERSIDE'S APPROACH TO HOME–SCHOOL LIAISON *Alwyn Morgan*

The reorganization of Hull schools, implemented in September 1988, heralded a significant development in the field of home–school liaison for Humberside LEA. Forty-two primary home–school liaison teachers, with a 0.5 non-teaching commitment, commenced their duties in what were regarded as less advantaged areas of the city.

While the reorganization was being planned, past records revealed a certain degree of underachievement, matched by an adverse distribution of the traditional indicators of educational need. This was reflected in a smaller percentage of pupils than the national average looking to continue their studies into either the sixth form or further and higher education. This scenario was therefore addressed when plans were made for reorganization.

After extensive research and visits to other authorities, it was agreed that an effective compensatory response would be to provide the less advantaged primary schools with an increased level of staffing, to encourage an enhanced level of parental involvement. This acknowledged the precept that where parents value education and encourage and support their children as they progress through the system, standards can be raised. Home–school liaison teachers were therefore to facilitate a whole-school approach to this challenging task, by encouraging every teacher to reflect a parental and community dimension to his/her work. However, such changes of policy and practice do not come overnight, and they need to be nurtured slowly and carefully.

After reorganization of Hull schools, Grimsby schools underwent a similar exercise (in 1990), with the creation of a further fourteen similar posts. However, with the introduction of Local Managment of Schools (LMS), the vast majority of the schools, appreciating the benefits of this work, now pay for these posts themselves from the compensatory element of their LMS budgets. It should be noted that two of the smaller schools were unable to afford such positions and the posts were lost, while other schools in the authority, unaffected by any reorganization, have capitalized on their compensatory budgets to create home–school liaison posts. Consequently, despite contracting resources, the future of this work presently looks encouraging for Humberside.

In order to facilitate the initial impetus for this work, the following developmental strategy was adopted:

1   Hull home–school liaison teachers were provided with a twenty-one-day training course. This initial input has been followed up by an on-going series of training events that respond to topical issues.

2   A network of mutual support groups for home–school liaison teachers has been established across the county, to provide a forum of discussion that is probably not forthcoming in their respective staffrooms.

3   Headteachers are regarded as the key agents of change and have consequently been kept abreast and informed of all new initiatives and also involved in a range of training events. Additionally, Grimsby headteachers meet on a half-termly basis to explore the managerial implications of the work.

4   As a whole-school approach is expected, this commitment must also be reflected by the education department itself. Consequently, some advisers and advisory teachers have been instrumental in supporting class teachers to see the parental dimension of their work.

5   Finally, in order to co-ordinate the home–school strategy, a specific post was created at a departmental level to provide guidance and support for all schools. Such has been the success of this work that an assistant has already been appointed.

In response to the above support structure, the initiatives from the schools may loosely be categorized as follows:

1   *A welcoming atmosphere* has been encouraged, to respond to the unease many people feel when visiting schools. This situation has been addressed with a variety of strategies, such as home visits, improved written communication and the establishment of community rooms. This last facility is used for a range of parent activities.

2   *Pre-school provision* has mushroomed. Considerable support has been forthcoming from social services under-5s officers and the Pre-school Playgroup Association. The latter has run numerous training courses for parents, which have been a cornerstone in the success of this work.

3   *Parents as educators* has been one of our major thrusts for development. Teachers have sought the good will of parents to reinforce, at home, the on-going work of the school. Parents and children work together on small tasks in many curricular areas. We believe that this approach will contribute to the raising of educational standards.

4   *Education as a lifelong process* has been encouraged through effective links with many providers of continuing education. Consequently, many community rooms host adult education classes for parents. Some parents have also studied GCSE courses in local high schools alongside daytime students. It is hoped that where pupils see education to be important to their parents, it will also take on greater significance for them.

5   *Curriculum development* is being facilitated by utilizing the skills and interests of people other than teachers, and placing greater emphasis upon community-related themes.

6   *Inter-agency collaboration* has been another significant plank for development. Many organizations in the voluntary and statutory sectors share an interest in the families that we work with. Consequently, collaborative action can enhance standards of care.

7   *Community development* has been encouraged. This takes many forms, such as over-40 parent netball teams, over 50s clubs, school and neighbourhood watch schemes, new clubs and societies, and greater dual use of school facilities.

A consultancy report produced by Tony Jeffs of Newcastle Polytechnic in July 1990 outlines many positive outcomes of Humberside's home–school liaison strategy. However, most importantly, we believe this work enables us to improve the quality of service offered to pupils, parents and community. Already schools are benefiting from a more positive profile, increased credibility, and growing good will from parents and local community.

While it is acknowledged that Humberside's home–school approach was initially based on a compensatory model, the Education Reform Act and other recent political edicts have ensured that effective liaison with parents should become a matter of major importance. The authority's position now is that all schools should involve parents and that all teachers should reflect this in their work. Unfortunately, too many teachers find it difficult to disengage the compensatory label from home–school work and see no reason to change their traditional practices.

Given that this approach now becomes expected of all teachers, there is an immediate need for training, which to date has been exceptionally conspicuous by its absence. This matter needs to be rectified quickly to enable teachers to adapt to this work confidently. Another timely issue is that of secondary home–school links. This phase of education has been notoriously complacent regarding the need to involve and communicate effectively with parents. Its shortcomings in the past will need to be addressed with due haste.

Finally, the attitude of the headteacher has always been crucial in determining the effectiveness of liaison with parents. With the diminishing role of the LEA and the increased powers of heads and governing bodies, particularly in the context of LMS, the major challenge in responding to the growing influence of parents must lie in headteachers' hands. This is an issue that should not be overlooked, as the quality of the future of our education service is at stake. Schools and parents need to work together confidently. Now, more than ever, headteachers must respond to this crucial challenge.

NEWHAM PARENTS' CENTRE: PARENTS AS PARTNERS IN EDUCATION *Ray Phillips*

We have consistently recognised the enormous pressure on the Local Education Authority. Yet although we know that a borough like Newham needs financial resources and educational plant, we have learned that a real and often unrecognised resource is the parent. (Newham Education Concern, 1974: Application for funding)

Seeds for the Centre were sown by a group of less than a dozen parents meeting together in the spring of 1973 to express concerns about the standard of education in Newham, a working-class Dockland borough in the East End of London. From this exclusively voluntary, non-professional base, relying on anxiety as the engine, we have moved over eighteen years to corporate structures. We now have a charitable programme engaging hundreds of volunteers, supported by thirty mainly full-time staff, on an annual budget of about half a million pounds, and a retailing education shop open six days a week and turning over about a quarter of a million pounds each year.

At the outset, we were organized as a non-charitable pressure group

(Newham Education Concern) with the general aim of 'improving by all possible means the quality of education in Newham'. As such, we were perceived as a threat by the LEA, who declared that the dissemination of educational information and promotion of reading help (two of our major concerns) were properly the responsibility of the education office, not to be shared with a street-level organization of parents. Attempts to secure local government funding for a parents' centre and education shop were unsuccessful.

With the help of Trust finance in 1975, we moved into a charitable framework (Newham Education Concern Services Association) to develop education services in priority areas identified by the pressure group, notably under-5s, reading help and careers support. This range of concerns neatly covered the 'school career' of a child and, therefore, attracted a large number of parents. An early structure was established for the production of publications and convening of meetings. Funding enabled us to set up a Parents' Centre in the Docks area, where we hoped to encourage parental involvement in schools. Just as teachers looked to the local Teachers' Centre for support and encouragement, so we intended to offer similar strategic back-up for parents.

As a local registered charity, we were able much more easily to develop a close working relationship with the Newham LEA to:

- seek and publicize information on education;
- involve, support and encourage parents to become better informed about and involved in our children's education;
- raise and realize parental/adult expectations through learning;
- involve volunteers in projects to help with particular educational problems.

The style was one of mutual aid rather than individualistic service. The organization was open to adults living or working in Newham, with an annually elected committee of management.

The home–school partnership is essentially a pious dream unless the status of the parent as an educational partner is deliberately fostered. No matter how disillusioned teachers may feel, working-class parents in an area of 'minimal schooling', such as Newham, share many negative experiences of 'education'. A dynamic partnership implies self-esteem for both partners. The alternative is co-option and subjugation! We appreciated this at an early stage of development.

Even before we opened the Centre, we were alarmed at how difficult it was to buy durable play materials and children's books in our inner-city area. How could we offer educational continuity for our children between home and school if there was no prospect of introducing educational materials into the home? School supply is effectively privatized by the teaching profession through inaccessible catalogues which rarely, if ever, see the light of urban day. We were annoyed at being forced to go into the centre of London to acquire appropriate

materials for a children's summer holiday play-scheme. Consequently, a key feature of the Centre is a street-level education shop
retailing children's books (rag, board, picture, story, multilingual) as
well as an extensive adult range (community, adult literacy, women's,
careers, reading schemes, revision aids, classics, etc.). The structure
to make this possible is a trading company limited by guarantee –
Parents Centre Activities (Newham) Ltd – established in 1978.

This community-based model of an education shop ensures that
parents as well as teachers can have access to educational materials. At
the same time, adults can enter the Centre to browse without running
the risk of being stigmatized as 'having a problem', which might well
be the case if we led with an 'advice centre' profile. Some parents will
return several times before they are willing to engage in a conversation
that will lead to their asking for specific help. To underpin our credibility in this latter regard, we have continued to produce a range of
educational publications. This independent 'intelligence' base is most
obvious in the form of our Newham Education Guide, where over 400
questions are answered on 100 topics. Although the LEA has advised
on the text, the responsibility is 'properly' taken by the Centre.

Apart from the education shop, our activities are targeted via eleven
sharply focused projects:

- *Going Community* – encouraging parental involvement as part
  of community education through the 24-hour-a-day Education
  Helpline, termly *Nexus* education newsletter, servicing
  Newham Association of Parent Governors and a local branch of
  the Workers' Education Association.
- *Parent Support Network* – ensuring that parents get their rights
  and meet their responsibilities under the 1981 Education Act,
  via parental guidance/advocacy for children undergoing
  assessment.
- *Breakinground* – support for adults with learning difficulties via a 2-year training course on gardening and landscaping
  with life and social skills back-up (accredited by City and
  Guilds).
- *Reading Help* – free help for adults with reading, writing and
  number through a wide range of learning styles and materials.
- *Pacer* – (Parents and Children Enjoy Reading) – a family-based
  approach to improving skills in reading, writing and number,
  with enjoyment as the key.
- *Young Families* – broad support for families with children
  under 5, via activities such as setting up parent and toddler
  groups, day trips, social events and holiday schemes.
- *Pre-vocational Training* – part-time day courses for unemployed
  adults (especially women returners) seeking introductory work
  skills (notably office/keyboard and parenting/childcare), with

generous life and social skills support as well as help with reading, writing and number.

- *ATAC* (Access Training Advice Centre) – for unemployed adults seeking guidance as to relevant local training opportunities at preparatory or more advanced levels in further education.
- *Open Learning Centre* – free guidance and study for adults wishing to improve basic skills such as reading, writing and number, via drop-ins, appointments, personal tutors, groups and courses, as well as self-help using computers.
- *Community Counselling* – an opportunity for adults to take stock of their own personal situation, especially in the light of educational or training provision.
- *Community Publishing* – encouraging local authors to get into print.

The durability oe our projects lies not only in their internal coherence but also in their developing interrelationships. This durability is reflected in the promotion of new ideas and activities as well as in the involvement and movement of volunteers. In this important respect, the Centre is based on the premise that a parent is the first generalist and the first volunteer. Parent participation assumes a 'dual interest':

- parents helping children (social engineering);
- parents helping themselves (adult education).

Over eighteen exciting years this has been the driving force behind our parental involvement strategy.

STARTING OUT: ESTABLISHING EFFECTIVE PARTNERSHIPS WITH PARENTS *Sue Miller and Jean Robinson*

In Northumberland, a multiprofessional team working in consultation with parents has been considering ways of developing policy and practice to facilitate more effective home–school liaison in the early years. Through discussion and consultation, a range of approaches, examples of good practice and support materials is being devised to help schools and parents to develop their current partnership.

In response to an open invitation within the authority, a group of some twenty to thirty people drawn from education, medical and social-work backgrounds began to meet together and consult with parents in Northumberland. The members of this group shared a common interest in and commitment to developing the links between parents and professionals in order to help children in all aspects of their development, particularly in the early years.

141

The main aim of the project was to produce a manual suitable for use in all first, primary or nursery schools, containing materials to help them to develop their relationships with parents. The project team always has been and continues to be committed to notions of a whole-school approach to this area. Effective relationships with parents, it is believed, depend very much on the affective nature of the inter-actions between the parents and teachers. The materials, therefore, concentrate on the 'how' of this developing relationship and the setting conditions for open positive dialogue between home and school.

Over eighteen months, and in their own time, members of the working party met together, mainly in smaller groups. Their primary objectives were:

1   to agree on some working practices or basic principles which were felt to be likely to facilitate effective home–school links;
2   to improve the first impressions which schools give through their buildings, personnel and community links;
3   to examine ways of celebrating and recording the achievements of children through a positive transferring and sharing of information between home and school;
4   to consider helpful ways of dealing positively with sensitive issues;
5   to outline ways of informing parents about and enabling them to take an active part in their children's learning;
6   to develop parent activity sheets describing the curriculum being followed by the children in school, with clear, straightforward descriptions of how this might be reinforced at home, and giving targets and small step objectives in each area;
7   to provide an action plan for developing a whole-school policy for establishing a partnership-with-parents policy.

As the project has developed, the working party has increasingly demonstrated that many aspects of this partnership are facilitated if these primary objectives are given close attention and carefully planned within an individual school.

A working document entitled 'Starting Out', some 200 pages in length and covering each of the sections described earlier, was available to all nursery and first schools from the end of 1991. While a clear framework for action is given, the emphasis of all the resources is very much on the *process* of this developing relationship, so that schools can individualize them to their own particular situations.

As with many such initiatives, the discussion with and development of individual members' understanding of the area under scrutiny have been at least as important as the finished document for these people. The group has already recognized that there would be a value in taking teachers, using this manual, through a similar process. This inevitable next stage will need to be negotiated with an eye to all the other demands being placed on schools for training. It is to be hoped, however, that this document will contribute to such discussion. The working party aimed to develop a 'team' approach to the skill development of a child, believing that in this atmosphere it is more likely that parents who have been involved in on-going dialogue will feel that this is an active partnership to which both sides can make positive contributions to children's learning. This positive and supportive atmosphere, generated through mutual respect and acknowledgement of the individual skills of parents, teachers and other specialists, has already been shown to benefit children.

HOME–SCHOOL LIAISON: AN LEA APPROACH   *Ann Evans*

Over the past few years, Warwickshire has been a quietly innovative and creative authority in the field of home–school liaison, initiating and supporting projects rooted in a firm belief in and commitment to involving parents in children's learning. The Education Committee strongly believed that the educational progress of children is profoundly affected by the confidence of parents in their own skills, and by their understanding of the aims and methods of the schools. For too many parents school is still an unfamiliar and even threatening institution. One of the main tasks, the committee thought, would be to de-mystify the education system as a whole, for all parents.

In practice, this philosophy has nurtured the opening up of nursery and first schools, with staged admission programmes; relaxed morning entry times to encourage shared activity and dialogue between parents, teachers and children; greater informal contact; more parental involvement in the classroom; curriculum workshops and shared projects; shared assessment and target setting between parents, teachers and children; and a general focus on all contact and communication with parents about children's learning and development. Secondary schools and colleges are slowly moving from their traditional stance of 'information giver' to that of 'information seeker'. Some schools are beginning to consult parents about aspects of the school development plan, and are recognizing that although practice will change as children go through the system, the principles of home–school liaison remain the same. Special schools often have a 'special' relationship with their parents, and we frequently look to them for a lead in their depth of work with parents. In the process of annual review of a child's statement of special educational need, there has been genuine consultation and participation within a supportive, sensitive forum to ensure that all the child's and family's needs are met.

Although each institution will largely have developed in its own way, hopefully in response to its community, there are vital ways in

143

which the LEA can give a policy steer and provide the structure and means for dissemination and support:

- *INSET* In recent years there has been a programme of INSET aimed at examining the rationale and philosophy for working with parents. Teachers have found that sharing ideas and practice with colleagues from other schools has provided a means of sharpening their own understanding and encouraged the development of practice within the school. A focus on newly appointed headteachers and probationer teachers has targeted the support to the teachers who can benefit the most.

- *Pilot initiative: the responsive school* A small group of middle and secondary schools are working with class or tutor groups of parents in a forum which allows the parent voice to be heard. Group discussion means that parents feel supported and encouraged to hear other parents' views and experiences, and teachers can listen to the concerns and interests of the parents. Experience has shown that there is a greater likelihood of partnership with parents being achieved if parents have an opportunity to influence the school's thinking and practice.

- *Policy underpinning practice* All schools are being encouraged to review their policy and practice in home–school liaison. The review framework facilitates a process of discussion with teachers, parents and governors and provides a model for action to aid developments. It also provides the authority with the information it needs both to know what is going on in schools and to be able to target support where it is most needed. County guidelines for home–school liaison will support the schools further in this work.

- *Dissemination* The sharing of information and practice around the county has helped to support developments. A newsletter both encourages and gives recognition to practitioners, and identifies where teachers may get help and advice from other colleagues. An inspection survey on 'the community-related curriculum' further highlighted and promoted good practice.

- *Evaluation* There is now a growing bank of evidence, through inspectorial visits and surveys, that home–school liaison has a heightened profile in Warwickshire. Whole-school review has enabled often disparate initiatives to be assessed in relation to aims and principles and made more integral to general school planning. Evaluation of the pilot initiative on the 'responsive school' showed the general direction for schools to move in – towards greater consultation and more effective communication with parents.

- *Future plans* There is a continuing need to stress the value of review and whole-school planning of home–school issues linked to school development. Consultation with parents and responding to their views will be an on-going focus. In addition, there will be a major thrust on 'reporting to parents' within a framework of Records of Achievement. All the investment that schools have made in developing good relationships with parents will pay dividends in this area of their work. Supporting teachers to develop a meaningful partnership with parents will be a continuing challenge. Schools are often embarking on a rewarding but painful journey which appears to get harder instead of easier, as parents gain confidence in themselves and the school and openly share their perceptions. We hope to continue to realize the worthwhile gains that result from a growing partnership between home and school.

CHAPTER 11

Case studies of parental participation in schools

CHAPTER OVERVIEW

The case studies are as follows:

- Front Lawn First School, Hampshire: Audrey Evans, ex-Headteacher of Front Lawn First School;
- Moordown St John's Primary School, Bournemouth, Hampshire: Hugh Waller, Headteacher, Moordown St John's;
- Newall Green Infant School, Manchester: Marsha Grime, Headteacher, Newall Green;
- The Cambridge Literacy Project: Lynda Pearce, Advisory Teacher, Cambridgeshire LEA.

FRONT LAWN FIRST SCHOOL – A SCHOOL CURRICULUM AWARD WINNER 1991 *Audrey Evans*

A decade of parental involvement, hand in hand with democracy in the staffroom, began for me when I came to Front Lawn First School as headteacher in 1981. I came from a new, open-plan school with an 'open-door' policy; before that I had learned a lot about trying to give parents responsibility while working for Save the Children Fund playgroups department. Front Lawn was a poorly achieving school on a lower-working-class estate with no community facilities. The previous head had been autocratic; there was a 'NO PARENTS BEYOND THIS POINT' notice clearly displayed. Changes had to be made.

The early appointment of a senior member of staff with special responsibility for pre-school and parent education, the 'doorstep' courses provided by South Downs College Adult Education Department and the high priority I myself placed on community work soon fired the enthusiasm of the rest of the staff, who had wanted to change but did not know how. The gathering momentum eventually took us all further than I had dreamed – to a School Curriculum Award for a school 'at the heart of its community'. This was a school where every look at improving the delivery of the curriculum in the classroom took us back into pre-school and the community. Originally pragmatic and implicit, this eventually became part of the school's written policy and guidelines. Front Lawn First School became a high-achieving school.

Each step led to the next: the mother and toddler club gave rise to the playgroup; our new entrants' sessions became stylized into pre-school groups for parents and children, and home visiting. Visits from the new urban-aided library link spread from pre-school into school itself. Growing interest in books from both parents and children (and staff!) led to Homelink, our parent partnership in reading scheme. News of its success and of our rising standards soon spread the idea from us throughout the area. The tea-parties held for parents in my early 'getting to know you' days developed into 'get to know your new teacher' class events for parents, teachers and children to discuss the year ahead together, or to celebrate the end of a project. There 'new' parents were invited to come on outings or to help with time-limited, short-term projects. This gradually gave us a nucleus of committed, well-trained classroom helpers who went on to run most of the fund-raising events, help at sports days and eventually become parent-governors.

Regular open days, to which parents came in small groups to see a classroom in action, gave parents an understanding of what and why, and a chance to ask questions, to express doubts or satisfaction and really know how their own children were progressing and how they compared with the rest of the class. In spite of some initial doubts, the staff gained tremendously in confidence from this exercise, knowing themselves to be held in such esteem by the parents. It gave us an opportunity, too, to ask and act on their views.

Parents came to know us in friendship in the pre-school years. We all agreed that it was better to discuss problems while they were still small ones rather than wait until they grew large. Realization dawned that parents are educators too, and could have choice and bring influence to bear on the way the school was run; that both head- and class-teachers were available at the beginning and end of each day to discuss problems without any appointment being made; that real help and advice could often be given in time of major family problems.

Thus there grew mutual respect, trust and a willingness to compromise and work together. From time to time, initially to ask for further support from the LEA, progress was recorded and the benefits listed. We gained confidence from seeing it in documentary form as a whole-school approach. Increasingly the parents – mainly mothers – went on doorstep courses, and also on FE and AE courses; several became qualified playgroup staff, others improved the quality of their lives; many went on confidently into employment. They sang the praises of 'their' school and became our public relations department!

Unexpected bonuses to us were the growing ease of discussing special needs and behavioural problems, such discussions often being initiated by parents themselves after a classroom visit. Thus discipline improved and our referrals to the educational psychologist fell away. Fund-raising increased rapidly as it became 'our' school, and the staff had increasing job satisfaction. They were appreciated by both 'customers' and employers – they had the ability to gain promotion to and in other schools, not least because the delivery of the curriculum to a higher standard became increasingly possible.

Parents of pre-school children always express a wish that their child will do well at school. In areas like ours they often add, 'In fact we would like him/her to do better than us – I don't think me and his dad made the most of our schooldays.' Could it be that it is the school system itself that often gets in the way of this sincere ambition? With the kind of parental involvement and participation outlined above and in the rest of this book, I feel that as families grow in self-esteem they and their children become responsible members of the educational establishment. At Front Lawn the uptake of the various facilities reached 95 per cent, as more and more of them became willingly involved. To me this is real parent power.

SHARING EXPERTISE AT MOORDOWN ST JOHN'S *Hugh Waller*

Moordown St John's is a voluntary-aided Church of England primary school with around 400 rising 5–11-year-olds, situated in a residential area of north Bournemouth. For several years now the school has pursued a declared policy of parental involvement, as a consequence of a redefined philosophy and practice among staff, coupled with a reappraisal of parental expectations and attitudes about school. The creation of a systematic and well-planned array of involvement initiatives has been well received by the participants, having recently achieved external validation following a school inspection.

Over the past few years, school policy and practice in the spheres of encouraging children's reading, literacy support, psychological involvement and educational workshops has placed a rightful emphasis upon parental participation from the very outset. At this school the relationship in the process of parental involvement has evolved into one of partnership, involving full sharing of knowledge, skills and experience between teacher and parent. Known as 'sharing expertise' (Figure 11.1), it draws upon the spirit of Wolfendale's 'equivalent

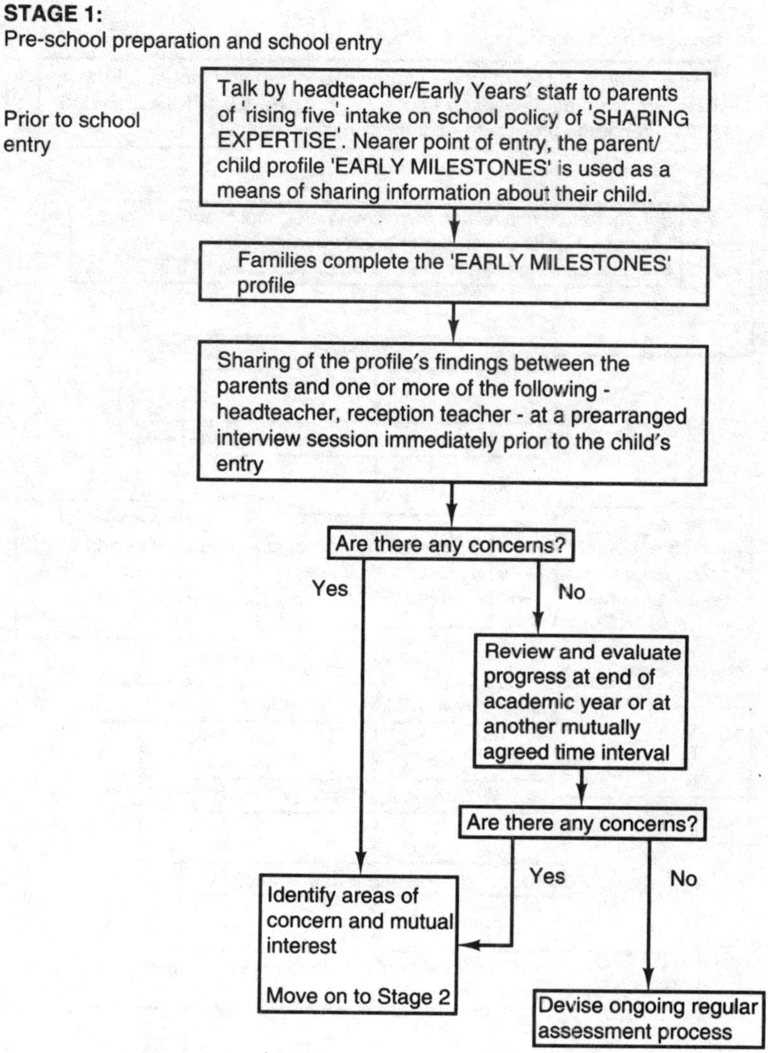

STAGE 1:
Pre-school preparation and school entry

Prior to school
entry

Talk by headteacher/Early Years' staff to parents of 'rising five' intake on school policy of 'SHARING EXPERTISE'. Nearer point of entry, the parent/child profile 'EARLY MILESTONES' is used as a means of sharing information about their child.

Families complete the 'EARLY MILESTONES' profile

Sharing of the profile's findings between the parents and one or more of the following - headteacher, reception teacher - at a prearranged interview session immediately prior to the child's entry

Are there any concerns?

Yes   No

Review and evaluate progress at end of academic year or at another mutually agreed time interval

Are there any concerns?

Yes   No

Identify areas of concern and mutual interest

Move on to Stage 2

Devise ongoing regular assessment process

Figure 11.1 Sharing expertise: an adaptation for Moordown St John's Primary School of a framework for co-operation between parents and professionals (originally devised by Sarah Goddard, 1988, from the 'equivalent expertise' model in Wolfendale, 1983)

STAGE 2:
In-house planned monitoring and assessment

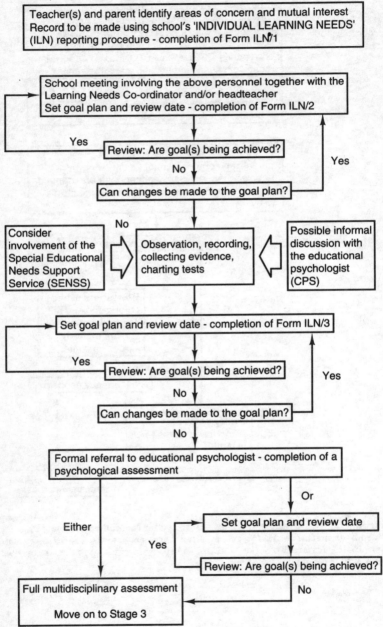

Teacher(s) and parent identify areas of concern and mutual interest
Record to be made using school's 'INDIVIDUAL LEARNING NEEDS'
(ILN) reporting procedure - completion of Form ILN/1

School meeting involving the above personnel together with the
Learning Needs Co-ordinator and/or headteacher
Set goal plan and review date - completion of Form ILN/2

Yes — Review: Are goal(s) being achieved?

No — Yes

Can changes be made to the goal plan?

No

Consider involvement of the Special Educational Needs Support Service (SENSS)

Observation, recording, collecting evidence, charting tests

Possible informal discussion with the educational psychologist (CPS)

Set goal plan and review date - completion of Form ILN/3

Yes — Review: Are goal(s) being achieved?

No — Yes

Can changes be made to the goal plan?

No

Formal referral to educational psychologist - completion of a psychological assessment

Or

Set goal plan and review date

Either — Yes — Review: Are goal(s) being achieved?

No

Full multidisciplinary assessment

Move on to Stage 3

STAGE 3:
The multidisciplinary assessment procedure and beyond

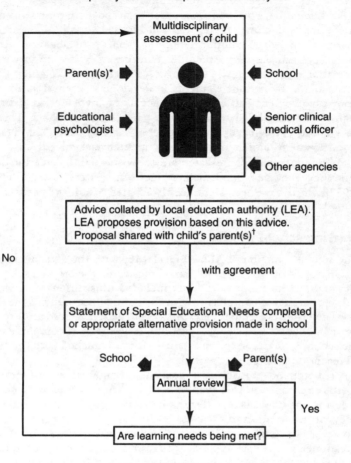

*Use is made of the parental profile *My Child ... My Story* in contributing to the multidisciplinary assessment of the child.

†There is an appeals procedure in the event of a parental disagreement with the Statement's advice.

Figure 11.1 *continued*

expertise' model (Wolfendale, 1983), while at the same time mirroring procedures in Dorset Education Authority.

For some time, a personal conviction of the positive gains to be made in children's learning when parents are actively involved as partners, sharing knowledge and information, has reaffirmed a belief in aiming to achieve mutual understanding. Working in co-operation with an educational psychologist, I have evolved a framework (Figure 11.2) to encapsulate the various elements in developing parental partnership from involvement initiatives. The levels of involvement naturally require investment of time by both parents and teachers. Through developing strategies for involving parents at each level, a movement towards parent–professional partnership has been evolved.

My involvement in a research project witnessed the creation of the following schemes, modelled on pioneering work by Wolfendale (1987), while have been significantly adapted to suit the needs of this school.

Starting school profile

The school's version of ALL ABOUT ME, with the agreement of its originator (Wolfendale, 1990), largely mirrored the original schedule, although, as an innovation, ours included illustrations as a way of helping parents to complete it with their child. Intended as a means of assessing the development and progress to date of a child prior to his/ her school entry as a rising-5-year-old, it was seen as complementing the school's 'sharing expertise' policy. It was launched with the 1989/ 90 reception intake.

A subsequent questionnaire analysis revealed an overwhelmingly positive response to this type of booklet, with may parents making observations like this one: 'I think it is an excellent way of conveying relevant information to the class teacher as well as being fun to do.' However, its format and appropriateness in certain sections were questioned by the vast majority who responded to the survey. It has to be borne in mind that Wolfendale's original profile had been aimed at children between 2½ and 6½ years old, who had come from a range of backgrounds and institutions, and who were being assessed for a wide variety of purposes.

The rationale behind this school's present pre-school profile, compiled jointly by a member of the school's infant staff and me (Brito and Waller, 1992), has centred on the need to be more precise and more pertinent to the needs of the reception teacher. In addition to a complete restructuring of the former profile itself, inclusions considered appropriate were:

- references to pre-school experience;
- activities which demonstrate the child's degree of hand control, knowledge of colours, ability to sequence pictures, level of

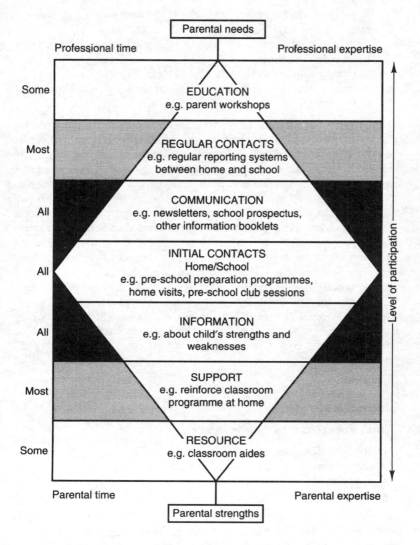

Figure 11.2 **Towards a model of parental–professional partnership (adapted from Hornby, 1989, by Goddard and Waller, 1990)**

vocabulary usage, general knowledge through naming pictures, and numeracy skills;

- highlighting those skills it is considered useful to have acquired upon entry to school;
- outlining a framework whereby parents could offer any additional information about their child which would ease transfer to the school.

Subsequent evaluation of written parental responses confirmed a feeling of involvement in their child's education through use of the booklet. For them, *Early Milestones* represented evidence of the school's concern to strengthen the home–school link, and to enable parents to offer a valuable contribution to their child's future schooling, as these questionnaire responses imply: 'made [my child] feel a part of the school before she joined ... also helps the mums to feel more at ease knowing that their child does not start school as a complete stranger', and, 'more valuable means of sharing information ... as things are often forgotten during parent/teacher interviews'. However, one has to be realistic and acknowledge that not all parents remain totally honest, preferring to present a biased profile of their child, a comment echoed by the reception infant staff. Nevertheless, they acknowledge the many advantages which have become evident, seeing the information collated from the profile as providing a baseline at point of entry. Not only does this value the child's previous experience by providing a brief snapshot, but also it highlights their record of development, achievement, progress, concerns and difficulties.

Literacy support

Taking due account of these principles:

- a willingness to share;
- identifying with one another's feelings;
- being genuine;
- mutual respect;

pursuit of the 'sharing expertise' model (Figure 11.1), in the management of children with perceived learning needs, underlines a multiplicity of mutual tasks which are viewed as essential in this reciprocal partnership between parents and professionals. Through use of pre-printed report forms, emphasis is placed upon explaining, describing, exchanging views and sentiments, defining and agreeing a problem, formulating and agreeing goal plans and establishing agreed review intervals. It also has regard for the language used, with minimum use being made of jargon, and clear explanations being given.

External validation followed a recent LEA school inspection, which included the following comments in the report: 'the strategies for learning support are well-planned ... a feature of this work is the high level of collaboration between home and school . . . the school's work in this area is outstanding.'

Parent profile at the multidisciplinary assessment stage

The pioneering work by Wolfendale (1988) in this area has subsequently been reaffirmed in DES circular 22/89 (DES, 1989):

> Parents, and the child, where practicable, should be helped and encouraged to participate in the assessment of the child's SEN as the 1981 Act envisaged. Frankness and openness between parents and the providers will help the process significantly, whereas the absence of parental co-operation is likely to delay assessment. (para. 21)

This led me, in partnership with an educational psychologist, to devise an adaptation of Wolfendale's 'guidelines for writing a parental profile' (Wolfendale, 1988), entitled *My Child . . . My Story* (Goddard and Waller, 1990), which is currently in use within the Dorset Education Authority.

The factors which guided us in the construction of the two parental profiles (for the pre-school/reception-age child and for the school-age child) have been:

- an absence of rigid questions and answers or an itemized format, which might inhibit the presentation of a creative response from parents, thereby suppressing valuable information;
- ensuring, conversely, that the guidelines are not so loose as to diminish their value as pointers and in providing structure;
- employing language that encourages parents to report the described behaviour in *observable* terms, yet also allowing free expression of feelings and impressions about the child;
- an acceptable *readability level* (assessed at the 8–9-year-old level) in the construction of guidelines, together with the inclusion of logos to reinforce key message points;
- exercising brevity both in the instructions and in the various profile components;
- the deliberate use of a user-friendly writing style which not only values the key role played by parents but also offers a continual channel of communication with the involved key professional (that is, the assigned educational psychologist responsible for initiating the multidisciplinary assessment).

Early responses to the use of these profile booklets are proving extremely favourable, confirming the authority's commitment to ensuring a sympathetic approach and developing a co-operative relationship with parents.

With the main thrust of the recent legislative change – open enrolement, Local Management of Schools – encouraging parents to consider themselves as consumers within the education marketplace, a school's procedures in developing meaningful and appropriate partnership strategies for home–school links are now crucial. Parents have continued to appreciate the links with this school at the pre-school stage. Plans are under way to evolve a package of materials for use by the pre-schooler (and his/her parent) within the home setting, which will create a more consistent link in the months leading up to the child's admission. The other reported initiatives have received external validation and continue apace, while further initiatives that will further strengthen the parent–professional partnership here have yet to be crystallized.

REFERENCES

Brito, J. and Waller, H. (1992) *Early Milestones*. Cambridge: Letterland.

DES (1989) *Revision of Circular 1/83 Assessments and Statements of Special Educational Needs: Procedures within the Education, Health and Social Services*. Circular 22/89. London: HMSO.

Goddard, S. and Waller, H. (1990) *My Child . . . My Story*. Dorchester: Dorset Education Authority.

Hornby, G. (1989) A model for parent involvement. *Network*, October, p. 2. Published by CEDC.

Wolfendale, S. (1983) *Parental Participation in Children's Development and Education*. London: Gordon & Breach.

Wolfendale, S. (1987) *Primary Schools and Special Needs: Policy, Planning and Provision*. London: Cassell. 2nd edition 1992.

Wolfendale, S. (1988) *The Parental Contribution to Assessment*. Developing Horizons No. 10. Stratford-upon-Avon: National Council for Special Education (now the National Association for Special Educational Needs).

Wolfendale, S. (1990) *All About Me*. Nottingham: Nottingham Educational Supplies.

ADDRESSES

Personal Services Branch, Dorset County Education Department, County Hall, Colliton Park, Dorchester, Dorset DT1 1XJ.

CEDC, Lyng Hall, Blackberry Lane, Coventry CV2 3JS.

Nottingham Educational Supplies, Ludlow Hill Road, West Bridgend, Nottingham NG2 6HD.

PARENTAL INVOLVEMENT AT NEWALL GREEN INFANT SCHOOL *Marsha Grime*

I had the privilege of being the first home–school liaison teacher in Manchester, funded by Urban Aid in 1975. The aim of the project was to involve parents actively in their children's education. Work from the Head Start and High/Scope projects in America has proved that good parental involvement in schools does make a difference, and the combination of good teaching with sensitivity to and valuing of the local community promotes positive attitudes to learning in children and adults. I am convinced that this process develops in parents a life-long commitment to their children's education and provides them with opportunities to improve and develop their own skills.

I came to Newall Green Infants as a new headteacher, full of enthusi-asm and determination to make parental involvement a priority. The staff in school already had good relationships with parents, but in the traditional teacher–parent style. Thankfully, they were a committed group of people who had their own children and knew the pressures on young parents. They showed a great willingness to work with parents in a way they had not done before. Parents were now welcomed, not challenged, and we knew it was important for all adults working here to have a clause in their job descriptions stating the importance of the parental work.

We started with small initiatives; for example, inviting parents to bring their children right into classrooms in the morning instead of waiting outside. A termly magazine soon followed, bursting with chil-dren's work and information about the school and its curriculum. When the staff defined the school aims, parental involvement was an essential element. The success of the initial contacts with parents encouraged further commitment; after two years the school had a part-time home–school liaison teacher, and we had become part of a project involving a community worker on site.

Six years on, the school is a stimulating and exciting place to be in. Some of the original staff have moved on, but the fundamental princi-ples of commitment persist as part and parcel of the day-to-day life of the school. Our work with parents goes from strength to strength, in many respects because of the feedback, support and many initiatives coming from the parents themselves. The following is a compilation of what goes on at school.

Teachers plan to spend a considerable amount of time with parents. They invite them into the classrooms every morning and evening. Within the setting of an integrated day, parents then help their chil-dren with reading, writing or a story. Not everyone stays to do this every day, but the option is there, and it is valued by both parents and staff. We hold weekly class assemblies to which parents are invited. Afterwards they have coffee with the class-teacher. These informal contacts facilitate later class-based workshops dealing with the cur-riculum, and the more formal parent–teacher interviews, when par-ents have the opportunity to spend time with the class-teacher on a one-to-one basis, sharing information about the child, discussing pro-gress and agreeing on recommendations for the future.

An unwanted classroom has been designated as a family room. (All of our families using it are visited by the home–school liaison teacher before the children begin school.) Pre-school activities such as toddlers' groups, playgrounds and crèches are based there. It is a bright, cheerful room where parents display their children's work. There is a weekly women's group, with activities organized and planned by the women themselves. They deal with issues such as health, food, sports, etc., and also involve themselves in projects around school. One such was their idea to redesign our school library. Over many months they reallocated the library, redecorated the room, made soft furnishings, checked books for suitability (gender, race, etc.), made visits to libraries and somehow managed to talk people into giving us lots of books. The end result is a really bright, cheerful library which both children and parents are proud of. At the opening ceremony everyone involved was presented with certificates for their efforts. Our parental education tutor supports adult learning by encouraging parents to attend courses both at school and at the local college.

Staff also organize events specifically for parents, sometimes to fund-raise, but mainly for pleasure. This year the nursery staff have organized community lunches with an international flavour. These have been really well received. When we have special events for the children, the parents are always welcome. They willingly take part and help out, making the occasion a memorable one.

We have several large information points for parents strategically placed around school. Information varies from 'bikes for sale' to 'welfare benefits for families'.

In the past year we have encouraged parents, governors and lunchtime organizers to join staff in in-service training. This has taken place after school (crèche supplied). The areas covered so far are peace in the playground and expectations of children's behaviour. The sessions are not only informative, but very enjoyable. Parents and staff discuss contentious issues freely, giving excellent feedback. Because there are good relationships between ourselves and parents, sometimes people in difficulty confide in staff. Using our close links with local support services, we do our best to get the help families need.

This has been only a taste of the variety of ways we involve parents. Our commitment is backed by Manchester City Council policies. The Adult Service has had the insight to provide the resources for the parental tutor, who works with parents, and our Chief Education Officer Roy Jobson's personal interest in parents is evident in his recently written parents' charter.

I have some concern about the DES admissions policy, which could force us to put classes in the family room and library, changing the character of the school and making work with parents more difficult. Finance difficulties at city council level might cut the PET role, and the school itself has a deficit budget this year. Life is becoming more difficult these days, but parents will always be a priority at this school.

PARTNERS IN LITERACY: THE CAMBRIDGE LITERACY PROJECT *Lynda Pearce*

As the Advisory Teacher for Reading within the Learning Support Team of the Cambridge area of Cambridgeshire, I instigated a local parental involvement project. Children were selected according to their needs and came from a wide variety of backgrounds. The emphasis was on supporting the teachers and parents of children experiencing difficulty with the processes of reading and writing. Several of the children were not experiencing severe problems, but still required positive intervention to enable them to become better readers, while others were experiencing severe difficulties with specific areas such as retelling stories, applying flexible reading strategies, comprehension, spelling or the beginnings of writing. Many were helped as part of a wider school project, and others were referred to either specialist teachers or educational psychologists for advice on appropriate, individual, parental involvement programmes. The children varied in age and ability, and a variety of approaches were utilized including shared and paired reading, pause, praise and prompt, simultaneous oral spelling and handwriting.

Initially a time scale of six weeks was set, but this was often extended when parents wished to continue. As the work was individualized and varied, it was impossible to produce quantitative results. However, the increase in the children's enthusiasm for and enjoyment of books, their pleasure in writing and confidence in sharing both reading and writing with their parents were clearly visible. Children who had been late in starting to read began to read and re-read picture books with their teachers and parents, and others who found building a sight vocabulary around the story a problem were helped with extra activities around the text.

Several of the parents were videoed working with their children on the selected areas, and these videos were used to train other parents and to help with in-service training in schools. A teachers' manual was written to guide teachers in starting projects with parents, and photocopiable booklets were written for parents to use as support material at home. The material was published in 1989 by Learning Development Aids as *Partners in Literacy*. This material is now being updated to include more specific work with parents on such topics as rhymes, and phonemic awareness activities around the reading and writing processes.

As the project developed, more and more schools were interested in instigating their own parental involvement programmes. This has led to the development of school-based 'parents as tutors' programmes over a period of one or two terms, covering all aspects of literacy. Parents now attend school for ten or more sessions per term to work with me and a special needs support teacher, head- or class-teacher. Initially, the parents were asked about any problems that might exist when working with their children at home. This acts as a counselling session and encourages the parents to discuss any of their own anxieties and fears about their child's progress in school. Parental anxiety often contributes to children's anxieties about their own progress in the development of reading and writing. This first meeting raises many issues which require sensitive handling prior to more in-depth training. Parents need to be encouraged to praise their children and to see themselves as facilitators to their children's learning, rather than teachers or tutors.

The sessions run in school for approximately two hours, before the end of the school afternoon. This enables the parents to collect any younger children at the end of the school day. Several schools now have a crèche available for very young children to attend while the sessions are held. Young children are too easily distracted and difficult to amuse while the parents are working with the teachers or children. The first four sessions cover the areas of telling and retelling stories, one-to-one correspondence, helping children with initial letter sounds and rhymes, and the beginnings of reading and early writing development. Parents are encouraged to see the links between listening, speaking, reading and writing, and to think of the processes as developmental and meaningful. Later sessions cover listening to children read in a positive way, paired reading, comprehension, the writing process, composing, drafting and editing, spelling and handwriting.

The parents are introduced to the topic during the first part of the session and are then supported while working with their own child for the second part of the session. They are encouraged to work with their child for a few minutes each day prior to the next tutoring session the following week. This method enables the tutors to observe the relationship between the parents and children as they work together, and to demonstrate any particular points that might need clarifying. This demonstration, practice and feedback approach works very well, as it allows for any practical problems to be dealt with when they arise, prior to the parents working with their child at home.

The second term is spent consolidating the approaches and ideas introduced during the first term. Parents are interviewed individually and are asked to evaluate the programme. These trained parents are then invited to train new parents the following year, and also to work regularly in school. In one such school, there are now six trained parents working in school with other parents, and also in classrooms with children experiencing difficulties with reading and writing. During the third term of the school year, meetings are held regularly, to discuss the parents' progress as they continue to work with their own child, and also to direct the work they are doing in school.

Many schools in the Cambridge area are now instigating their own parental involvement projects, using this material as a resource, both for individual children with difficulties and for larger group and school projects. As teachers we are concerned with the development of the whole child, so what we do in school must be related to life out of school. Any project that fosters home–school links, encourages the family to work together and promotes the development of literacy must be worth the efforts involved. The emphasis throughout must be on enjoying learning. Most parents are very good at making learning situations fun, and, given the correct guidance from the school, can be true partners in their child's literacy development.

Name Index

Subject Index